ABOUT THE AUTHOR

Warren Page has served for nearly 20 years as Gun Editor of FIELD & STREAM. Born in New England and educated at Harvard University, Page was a World War II Navy officer assigned to gunnery research and instruction. He has hunted nearly every kind of game on six continents; was the first hunter in more than 50 years to bag a rare blue or glacier bear in Alaska; the third American to take a bongo antelope in French Africa, and has contributed nine heads to the Boone & Crockett Club North American Big Game Records. In 1958, Page received the top prize of big-game hunters, the Weatherby Trophy. An expert marksman, he holds several national championships and a world record. Also a ballistics expert, Page developed the 6 mm cartridges adopted as the .243 Winchester and the .244 Remington. Married and the father of two children, Page lives at Chappaqua, New York.

THE FIELD & STREAM GUIDE TO

DEER HUNTING

BY
WARREN PAGE

HOLT, RINEHART AND WINSTON, INC.

383 Madison Avenue, New York, N.Y. 10017

1966

FIELD & STREAM

GUIDE TO

DEER HUNTING

CONTENTS

CHAPTER 1

Our Number One Big Game Animal

Hunting has grown faster in recent years than any other participant sport. Hunters outnumber golfers nearly three to one, for example. In the past two decades, while our population has increased by 43 percent, the number of hunting licenses sold has jumped by 80 percent. The hunter pours over 1.5 billion dollars a year into our economy, and drives five billion miles a year for his sport. Over 40 million American households contain firearms, and close to 20 million Americans hunt each year.

Of course not all of these are big game hunters. Probably less than half, but the number of red-capped males (and over a million gals are licensed every year) who hunt for game larger than one hundred pounds, if you'll accept that as a definition of big game, is still legion. And the vast bulk of them are, or certainly start out as, deer hunters.

TWO MILLION DEER A YEAR

In the year 1964, this sizeable army shot 1,095,570 whitetail and, if we lump mule deer and the closely related Columbian blacktail together, 838,157 of the long-eared western species. That's 1,933,727 deer. When we consider that 11 states, of which several hold regular whitetail seasons, but do not report, the total annual deer kill must run far above 2,000,000 head!

That more deer are taken by sportsmen than all other large game animals added together is no surprise. Six times as many, in fact. The deer may not be our most difficult big game animal, though that is open to argument; nor our most handsome game animal, though that too might be debated. And deer could hardly be termed a dangerous game animal, though an incautiously approached wounded buck can raise havoc with sharp hooves and horns. But no one can deny that our two basic brands of deer, whitetail and mule deer, are the game animals most popular on this continent.

MORE DEER THAN PILGRIMS HAD

It is commonly observed that there are more whitetail today than there were when the Pilgrims landed. Since neither our Pilgrim fathers nor the resident redskins recorded game surveys, this statement has to be taken on faith. But it is undoutedly so, since all recent biological studies and experience demonstrate that the peculiarly adaptable whitetail deer develops peak herd density on acreage that has been repeatedly timbered over—even farmed—rather than in primeval or climax forest.

The type of wilderness that clothed the eastern, southern, and central states in Dan'l Boone's day would support relatively few deer because the towering trees choked out just those types of bushy browse that nourish deer, and flourish on cut-over lands. Since hunting was not controlled during the days of exploration, expansion, and settlement, it is not surprising that whatever the size of the deer herd when the white man arrived, that herd had been cut down to a minimum, was actually in danger of extinction by the end of the 19th century.

WHITETAIL MORE WIDESPREAD NOW

The nearly incredible comeback of the whitetail was signaled by conservation moves such as those of Pennsylvania, which then placed the species under full protection, a step followed by nearly all states either side of the Appalachians. Despite the growing density of human population, under reasonably efficient game management programs the whitetail has multiplied until an estimate of 10 million alive today is a conservative figure.

Over the same period, the white-sterned Virginia deer has extended his range over virtually the entire United States and all the Canadian provinces edging the border. One would hardly think of whitetail in Kansas, yet the population is now estimated to be above 20,000; plains states like Iowa, Nebraska, the Dakotas today boast even larger herds and have regular open seasons. The hunter in Washington now sees deer of a sort that a generation back he'd have expected to find no further west than Minnesota or Wisconsin. The same species of deer that nips off petunias in gardens outside Providence, Rhode Island, hardens his antlers on the mesquite brush of Texas. The only difference

The whitetail deer has a full, broad tail with pure white hair on under-surface. If danger threatens, tail stands erect like flag

is that "little Rhody" has only about 1,500 head while huge Texas boats 2.5 million. And the southwestern deer run a mite thinner and greyer in hair because of the milder climate. The whitetail deer, it can now quite properly be said, uses the entire United States for his range.

MULE DEER LOSING GROUND

Far less adaptable to human activities, unable to live happily in crowded suburbia the way whitetail can, the mule deer occupies a slowly but steadily decreasing range. At the time of Lewis and Clark, about 150 years ago, he spread out beyond the Rocky mountain foothills onto the great plains. But today, despite successful re-introduction into the Black Hills and such marginal areas, the mule deer is more and more being confined to mountain states like Colorado, Utah, New Mexico, western and southern Texas, Arizona, Nevada, Wyoming, Montana, Idaho, the western counties of Washington, Oregon, and California, where wide open spaces still exist and the mule-eared deer have high country as a summer rufuge.

MANAGEMENT PROGRAMS ASSIST MULEY

No dweller along town edges, the mule deer must slowly give way to forces generated by grazing, timbering, and mining interests, as well as other civilizing forces gnawing at the western states. In the narrow view, the mule deer is holding his own under management programs financed by the flood of license fee money his hunting provides the western states. But in the long-term view, his future in terms of available range seems questionable.

Yet to many, the tall and wide-spreading rack of the rubber-hooved mule deer makes him a far more handsome trophy that the delicate whitetail will ever be. A symbol of our mountain states, the muley is a prime hunting target; and as long as Colorado and Utah can maintain an annual take of well over 100,000 each, he will continue to be.

1937: 3,181,675

1958: 5,538,843

Whitetail deer population has made tremendous comeback since end of 19th century when animal was nearly extinct. Department of Interior figures, although not complete, show that deer count in U.S. rose from about three million in 1937 to more than five million in 1958, when census was discontinued. Experts now estimate population is near 10 million

11

CHAPTER 2

A Brief Natural History of the Deer

Biologists may argue the point, but as the hunter looks at them we have in this country two basic types of deer, the whitetail and the mule deer. Each has a secondary species more set off by the limits of its normal habitat than by any marked physical detail—the Coues deer of Arizona which is a small localized whitetail, and the Columbian blacktail, which is a mule-eared breed of the northwestern coastal states, British Columbia and lower Alaska. Whether or not the major and secondary species ever interbreed, as the muley with the blacktail, is still a hot argument among the scientists, though it has little meaning for the average hunter. Content to leave life uncomplicated, he usually thinks in terms of the two major species.

The whitetail, *Cervus virginianus* or *Odocoileus virginianus,* depending on the system of nomenclature you prefer, ranges today over virtually all of the United States, edging down into Mexico and spreading into the lower tier of Canadian provinces. Highly adaptable, it thrives wherever there exists adequate cover and browse, with winters no more than moderately severe. The most outstanding characteristic of the whitetail is the over-long tail, coated on the underside with long white hair. When raised in alarm or in curiosity, this long flag, enlarged by the erectile white hairs of the inner rump, is unmistakable as the source of the whitetail's common name.

ONLY BUCKS WEAR BASKETS

The antlers of the whitetail are shed each year between mid-December and early March, depending on conditions, and regrown each spring. They appear only on bucks save in rare instances of a doe with glandular malfunction. They are most graceful but peculiar in form, in that instead of developing in a series of forks off forks, the points of an adult male rise nearly vertically from the main antler beam. They sweep upward from the brow, then swing forward and around to give the rack a basket-like form.

Occasionally the antler bone may be malformed by accident while still soft, as it is during the late spring growing season. Sometimes multiple-point racks occur which can only be classed, for trophy purposes, as non-typical. Brow tines normally appear.

The adult breeding buck usually carries four or five points

Range of the whitetail deer extends through all of the 48 contiguous states plus Mexico and the Canadian Provinces from Nova Scotia and New Brunswick to British Columbia. It is highly adaptable and thrives in areas with adequate food supply and protective cover

on each side, hence is considered an eight or 10 pointer by the Eastern count. This takes into consideration as points all projections which are longer than they are wide at the base, and uses the combined total of both antlers. The number of points is a completely unreliable index of a whitetail's age. Local conditions will determine whether growing bucks at any given stage will carry merely forks or three points to a side, for example. The antlers of old bucks, gone beyond breeding capacity, often deteriorate.

Whitetail bucks battle quite savagely during the rutting period, which may begin at varying times between late September and early November, usually after two or three killing frosts. And the bucks often die tragically with their antlers enmeshed. In the Southwest, rattling antlers to produce their battle sounds is a useful ruse to draw the attention of other adult males.

AVERAGE WEIGHT ABOUT 140 POUNDS

The on-the-hoof weight of whitetail bucks varies from 100 to 300 pounds, depending on age and the nutritional elements of their local feed. Northern deer generally run larger than their southern brethren. The national average weight is probably 140 pounds on the hoof, or about 110 dressed.

A simple factor to convert known hog-dressed weight to live weight is to add 28 percent. Does generally run lighter in weight, though an old dry doe will scale out as heavy as a young forkhorn or three-point.

The fawns, usually twins when feed conditions permit, are dropped in late April or May. Almost scentless during their early helplessness, they carry spotted markings for most of their first year. The pelage, or coat, of grown deer is quite rufous, almost fox-red, in the summer months. But it turns steadily to grey—in the case of old bucks to a decidedly dark grey—as the winter coats are grown.

Whitetail are not grazing animals, though they will nip off the tender green shoots of winter wheat or rye, more generally browsing on a great variety of herbs, weeds, and the fresh shoots of deciduous trees. They turn to evergreens only under most desperate winter circumstances. The mast or nuts of hickory, oak, beech or hazel are preferred forage.

When frightened, the whitetail deer's tail flashes erect and it bounds for cover, it is a marvel of grace in leaping over a log

BUCK AND DOE TRACKS DIFFER

The whitetail gait when frightened is a bounding run with tail flashingly erect. But they will also creep or crawl very close to the ground, or stand for long minutes stock-still, only the nervous movement of the tail or an occasional ear-flick betraying their presence.

Determining which track is a buck and which a doe is as much intuition as reason. But the hoof of a heavy buck tends to splay more under his weight, the dew-claws more likely to print even at a walk. And the casually traveling buck in light snow often tends to drag his hind feet so they leave a swagger mark.

Creatures of habit and accustomed to living within a range as circumscribed as one square mile, whitetail feed early and late in the day, often feeding at night. They prefer to bed down during daylight hours, either in the center of the deepest spruce swamp available or, especially in the case of wary bucks, on a ridge point where signals to nose or eye come from several directions and as many escape paths are offered. The route from feeding to bedding area may be used so consistently that it forms a regular trail, when deer are not being hunted.

The gait of a white tail deer differs from that of a mule deer. A hard-running whitetail buck may cover 10 feet in a stride and the animal can easily make a 20-foot leap. It demonstrates an ease of motion; takes obstacles with little apparent effort

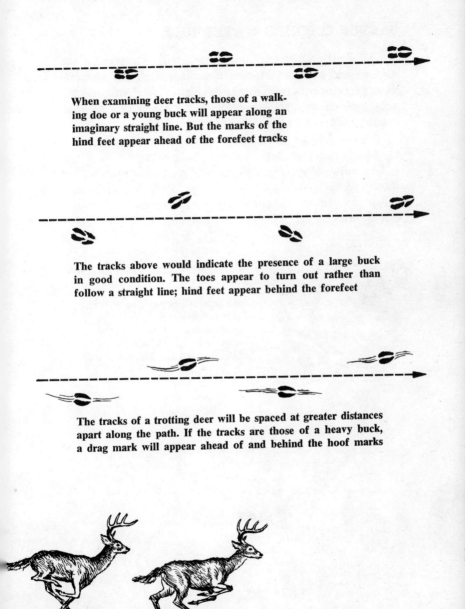

When examining deer tracks, those of a walking doe or a young buck will appear along an imaginary straight line. But the marks of the hind feet appear ahead of the forefeet tracks

The tracks above would indicate the presence of a large buck in good condition. The toes appear to turn out rather than follow a straight line; hind feet appear behind the forefeet

The tracks of a trotting deer will be spaced at greater distances apart along the path. If the tracks are those of a heavy buck, a drag mark will appear ahead of and behind the hoof marks

17

CACTUS IS COUES WATERHOLE

The Coues whitetail, earlier mentioned as peculiar to Arizona and northern Mexico, has adapted all the whitetail traits to a desert habitat. It has learned to water from cactus pulp, for example. Thin-coated in dove-grey, with a delicate but full rack, the Coues deer, for all his top weight approximates only 100 pounds. It is a spooky and difficult trophy for southwestern hunters.

The mule deer, also designated *Cervus macrotis,* is instantly recognizable from the long, pointed, mule-like ears, which save in the grandest old bucks are outsize for the rest of the animal. The antler form also is markedly dif-

Seen from the rear, the mule deer's tail is cylindrical in shape and lacks the bushiness of the appendage which gives the whitetail its name. Mule deer tail also has a black tip

ferent, branching in a series of forks so that a normal adult male is likely to carry four apparent major prongs, plus one brow prong or eye guard, on each side, and so be termed a five-point in western parlance.

The count may run either higher or lower, however, and abnormal or non-typical, many-pointed heads are fairly common in the mule deer clan. The mule deer's rump patch is a very pale tan or cream color. The tail, shorter than a whitetail's, has a black or dark tip.

Mule deer range at one time extended as far to the East as Minnesota but now is restricted to the high plains of Montana, the Dakotas, and Saskatchewan and the mountainous regions of the western U.S., Canada, and Mexico. The range map below also includes the Columbian blacktail deer which inhabits the Pacific Coast forests from California to Alaska

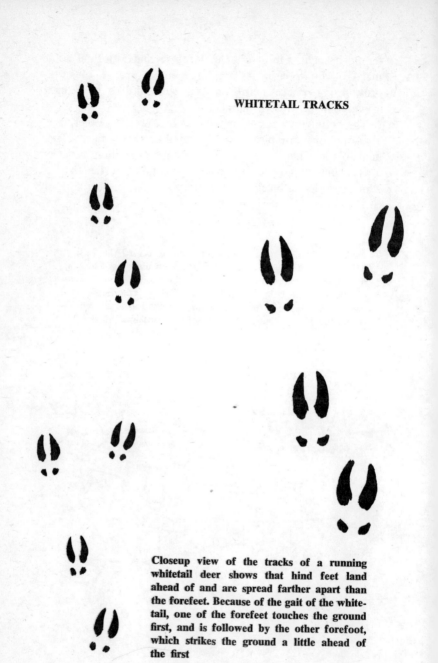

Closeup view of the tracks of a running whitetail deer shows that hind feet land ahead of and are spread farther apart than the forefeet. Because of the gait of the whitetail, one of the forefeet touches the ground first, and is followed by the other forefoot, which strikes the ground a little ahead of the first

The mule deer moves at a full gallop only in desperation. The usual gait is a series of rubber-ball bounds with all four feet closely bunched. Each leap is high enough to clear sagebrush

MULE DEER MAY WEIGH 200

Mule deer range, though it once extended far out onto the plains, still involves the drainages both east and west of the Rocky Mountains well out into foothill and desert country, from the Sierra Nevadas of Mexico and Baja California to about one-third of the way north into Alberta and British Columbia.

A much blockier and heavier-bodied deer than the white-tail, the mule deer may also stand taller, up to 40 inches or more at the shoulder. And while the average weight of the bucks is not markedly higher, perhaps 25 pounds more, many mule deer under rich feeding conditions will go over 200 pounds. Bucks have been reported as weighing over 300 when hog-dressed. The largest alfalfa-fed monster the writer ever shot weighed 279 pounds with the lower legs lopped off and insides removed. But such super-bucks are counter-balanced by the smaller types of the southwestern desert country.

Tawny in color during the warm months, the mule deer's coat in winter darkens to steel grey. The muzzles of old

The mule deer moves across the countryside by a series of stiff-legged bounces, much like a big rubber ball. His gait is well suited to the rough, broken terrain in which he lives. Because of this gait, the tracks of the mule deer show the feet bunched together, with the rear hooves slightly behind the front ones. The distance between sets of tracks may vary somewhat, being farther apart if the deer is moving downhill. Dew claws usually appear in the tracks if the animal is running hard

The antler of the mule deer has the general sweep of the whitetail's but the basal tine usually is smaller in proportion, except in some old bucks. The first upright tine is generally quite massive and may be thicker than the main beam

bucks, often surprisingly Roman-nosed, are quite decidedly black with white and grey markings. They are often the first feature seen in binoculars, as are the ears and shiny black muzzle of an inquisitive doe.

MULEY'S GAIT LIKE BALL BOUNCE

The mule deer gait is most distinctive. Using a full gallop only in desperation, their usual flight is a series of rubber-ball bounds, with all four feet closely bunched, bounding high enough to clear the average sagebrush. This makes for a most difficult target, but the mule deer rarely runs in this manner for any great distance.

Larger-hooved than the whitetail, the mule deer buck with the exception of the bouncing trace described above, leaves toe-drags in snow or deep sand when walking slowly, and in soft surfaces splays his hoof somewhat.

The Columbian blacktail, in Alaska referred to as the Sitka deer, is like his larger cousin in antler formation though much less massive. The world record typical blacktail head scores 160⅝ points as compared to 217 for the top mule deer known. It also has a short black-tipped tail, in this instance the black running clear up the outside with little hair at all on the underside. And much like the mule deer, it undergoes a seasonal change of coat from bay to grey. The blacktail's ears are slightly less mulelike. Its habits and habitat in thickly timbered regions of the northwest are, however, more like those of the whitetail than of the open-country mule deer.

Single hoof marks studied closely can help hunter to tell the type of animal he is trailing. Pressure of the hoof of a heavy buck or a hard-running animal causes a splayed pattern and the show of the dew claws. Distance between prints indicates gait of deer.

MULE DEER IS MIGRATORY

With all these deer, the normal fawn drop under good conditions is two, three being exceptional and one usually being the result of over-population or poor feeding conditions.

Where the whitetail tends to remain near its birthplace no matter what the wintering situation, the mule deer often tends to follow a migratory pattern by changing altitude from summer range around timberline and in the higher parks down onto the desert under pressure of deep snow and cold.

Columbian blacktail, which seeks cover in the heavy forests of the Pacific Coast, has antlers similar to those of the mule deer except that they are smaller and lighter in weight. The tail has a shape similar to whitetail but the upper surface is black

CHAPTER 3

Bagging the Wary Whitetail

It is hardly accurate to say that there are as many methods of hunting whitetail deer as there are Nimrods in red caps pursuing them. But there certainly are as many systems used as there are varieties of terrain or areas in which the Virginia deer are hunted. And every technique has its merits, depending on the cover to be hunted, on the number of men involved in the hunt, and, in very important degree, on the personalities of the hunters themselves.

Veterans of the whitetail woods generally have learned by long and bitter experience that a "slow and easy" approach to the problem of spotting a wary whitetail buck before he spots *you* is more likely to pay off in venison liver for breakfast. The great majority of deer hunters, however, and this is particularly true of Nimrods new to the sport, are much too brash, too impatient, for any such procedure. Their very nature demands a slam-bang attack. They cover miles in a day, walking rapidly, not only down rain-quiet tote roads but through the dense cover, half the time with their eyes down on rough ground, making racket enough to draw the attention of every buck in a quarter-mile radius. The smart old buck—and the smart old hunter—may well lie doggo until the noisy parade has passed.

Like his mule deer cousin, a whitetail buck may lie quietly in the brush, its antlers and hair blending with the leaves and branches, and be unnoticed by the noisy Nimrods who stumble through the forest

The stump-sitter must learn how and where to position himself so that he can see the deer before it spots him. This means avoiding a tree trunk in the middle of a clearing. The best place is close to a trail used regularly by whitetail, with the hunter's outline concealed

SOME ONLY SEE DEER DISAPPEAR

The fast-movers may actually see more deer in a day than anyone else. But the great majority of the deer they locate are already bouncing off in high gear. Bucks will stay put just long enough to identify the marcher as a man and a menace, then run toward safety so far ahead of the fast-mover that he sees only a white tail and stern flitting off disdainfully.

The hunter is offered either no shot at all or at best a chancy opportunity at a barely glimpsed target, one seldom surely identifiable as a buck anyway. The all-day hiker actually is the best possible assistant to the stump-sitters and quiet-movers, since the bucks he stirs up may well be pushed straight at them.

The sensible whitetail hunter bears in mind certain basic habits and qualities of the deer himself. First, whitetail are not wide-ranging game. They often live out their entire lives within one or two square miles. As a result, they know their home terrain intimately, down to the last square yard. They know the movements and noises normal to the area, are familiar with every spruce swamp or patch of heavy laurel cover, every path or trail that may serve as either an escape route or as an easy road from feeding to bedding ground and back.

Since beating the buck on his home ground by barging through the cover at full and noisy speed is doing it the hard way, wise whitetail hunters play the game the opposite way, by letting the buck come near them.

HOW TO STAY WARM DURING LONG WAIT

The stump-sitter clan probably scores highest in terms of bucks per man-hour, particularly in hard-hunted regions where the deer are being moved by other shooters—and most of all in limited areas where they can know details of the terrain as well as do the deer.

The chief limitation placed on the stump-sitter is his own ability to sit still—really still—and that in turn depends on his own patience and his own ability to withstand the creeping cold of late fall, during the time of hard frosts. The long-experienced stump-sitter has of course learned to use heavy wool or insulated underwear; to wear goose down or equivalent insulation on the outside; to tuck a couple of handwarmers under his heavy shirt, next his kidneys; to keep the feeling in his feet with multiple layers of socks in loose boots, with surplus flight boots or insulated rubbers.

He long ago found out that any hike out to his favorite sitting spot should be done slowly, with outer warm clothing left open or carried separately, since if his underclothing is dampened by a sweaty walk he'll almost inevitably be forced into movement after sitting only the first hour.

DON'T LET DEER SEE YOU

Even more important, the sitter must learn how and where to sit. Not for him the stump or convenient tree trunk in the middle of a clearing, from which he can see well in all directions. The deer can see him too, and any such prominent display defeats itself.

I have known of long-practiced sitters who have actually built blinds, have gone so far as to keep a lantern burning under blanketed knees to ensure warmth. But the blind, used chiefly to mask casual but revealing movement, is hardly necessary. The stump-sitter should, however, place himself so that he is at least partially hidden, his outline broken, where the buck will be both heard and seen during his approach.

Hence the sitting spot should be not on but next to a likely deer road or trail. As creatures of habit, whitetail regularly follow the same paths, hardly as well-defined as man-trails or cattle-paths, but light traceries through the forest, clear enough if any overlaying leaves are scraped off to leave the tracks in soft earth.

HOW TO FIND DEER TRAILS

The deer trail may wander with seeming aimlessness, but it will always follow the line of easiest travel or least resistance with two important exceptions. One is that deer, especially old bucks, like to move in protective cover. The other is that a deer trail, as distinct from the trace left by two or three men who have walked the same line, will go casually under tree branches or through close-set saplings that either men or woods-wandering cattle automatically avoid.

The sitter's hideout then should be near such a trace, preferably one that bears the signs of recent use, or better yet, near the intersection or junction of two such routes. The hunter should be able to see clearly in any direction 20 or 30 yards. The deer will be coming to the sitter, and, unless he has fallen asleep or has frozen his ears, he will hear the buck moving along well before the buck sees him. The deer may be coming fast if he has been surprised by other hunters, or picking along casually if he is feeding undisturbed.

Then it is up to the hunter, before the buck is actually in sight, to worm himself around and to raise his rifle part of the way to his shoulder. This maneuver will give the hunter more time to decide whether the rustling incomer is indeed a proper buck, not a doe or another hunter Indian-footing along the trail.

SLEEPERS GET RUDE AWAKENING

Many are the sorry tales of stump-sitters who fell asleep, or had buried their ears too deeply under cap and coat-collar, then suddenly realized that a whopper buck had slipped up unheard and had been watching them for minutes. The buck usually awakens such hunters with a loud snort and a whirling jump into heavy cover. The sitter must remain still and silent, but he must not fall asleep!

The same might be said of standers during deer drives, although most such drives, when properly planned to cover a limited section of cover, are of too short duration for that much relaxing.

Except for the situation peculiar to the southeastern states, where impossibly dense cover and a local tendency to support large-scale "social" hunts require packs of hounds to drive deer past waiting gunners, there are two basic driving methods.

MASS DRIVES IN HEAVY COVER

The first, common in many heavily hunted areas where perhaps two dozen hunters club up in a mass operation, is the noisy drive. This is a "blast-em-out" procedure, developed to a high art in the pinewoods of southern New Jersey. The group splits, each half of the gang operating as drivers and standers in turn. Once the standers have had time to deploy themselves along old roads or field edges to form a U on the downwind side of the area to be driven, the beaters or drivers come marching through in a line, hooting and hollering and kicking the brush to force any deer into panicky flight toward the standers.

The scheme usually works best in extremely heavy cover and is practiced most where state laws—for the obvious reason of safety—demand the use of shot-guns loaded with buckshot. However, it is frequently used, on a larger scale with greater spread between the drivers, in sections where rifles are legal.

The large noisy drive produces many deer, of course, but usually gives the standers only non-selective running shots. Other than the common problem of being difficult to organize effectively—because the hunter group often contains more would-be chiefs than ordinary Indians—the big drive has one major drawback. It may leak. In other words, the driver group may become so wide and thinly spread that smart old bucks, fully aware of the position of individual members of the drive because of their constant

32

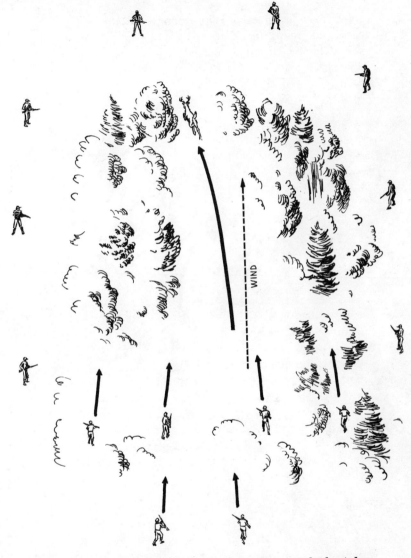

In some areas of extremely heavy cover, deer may be hunted with the mass drive technique. Half of the group of hunters serve as drivers who force the deer downwind toward the standers. The drivers kick the brush and shout to frighten the deer into the line of standers noise, may lie quiet or slip through the driver line. Experienced groups, therefore, often spot a pair or so of really skilled hunters to work along slowly as back-stops to the drivers.

A small group of hunters may bag their bucks by using a quiet drive technique in terrain that has been carefully studied. The object is not to frighten the deer but to move them slowly along routes that are so predictable that even the does and fawns can be sorted out

PUSH DEER GENTLY INTO POSITION

Better fun, and a better proof of both hunting skill and knowledge of terrain, is the quiet drive. It might better be termed the gentle push. A small hunter group of less than a dozen, perhaps only four or five, can work this system to perfection if they know the area well. The object is to move deer slowly, not to scare them into wild-eyed fright but to nudge them ahead of only two or three pushers along routes so predictable that they can be blocked by a few standers.

As a classic example of the very effective quiet drive, let's take a layout repeatedly successful in typical Catskill deer country. The area is a partial bowl, with a pond at the bottom, its northern edges rising onto a U-shaped ridge broken on the western side by a notch cut by deer trails. North of that notch rises a steep rocky slope cut by several brushy gullies, with faint deer trails side-hilling the slope below the notch.

The pushers—and two or three are sufficient—start from just south of the pond, wander through a swampy section of dense cover which under most circumstances hides deer bedded down for the day.

The standers are usually spotted in the following pattern: one south of the notch, one overlooking it, one atop the rocky steep where he can command one or two of the gullies as well as the bottom of the cliff, and one or two strung down along the sidehill trails between the steep slope and the lake edge.

QUIET DRIVE YIELDS BETTER TARGET

Repeatedly, this simple drive, done in absolute quiet and covering far less than a square mile of timbered terrain, produces the same result. The does and young deer move out of the bowl through the notch. The better bucks, smart enough to avoid the obvious route, either sneak along below the steep rocks, or eventually turn up through the rocky area in the cover of one of the well-brushed gullies.

At least three-quarters of the time, if there are deer in the swamp at all, it is either the stander atop the rocks or his neighbor toward the lake who gets a shot. And in a quiet drive that shot may well be at a standing or slowly moving deer, so that selection by antler quality or a dead-sure hit behind the shoulder are almost guaranteed.

On several occasions during this sort of drive, which can be adapted to nearly any whitetail cover, I have had deer move past far ahead of the pushers so undisturbed that they would even stop and feed. They've come close enough, so long as I remained motionless and they did not catch man-scent, to be poked with a long stick.

The man who sits and waits along a whitetail deer trail frequently scores as high as he who crashes through the brush in search of game. The stump-sitter must remain really still but stay alert for the wary buck

AVOID FLUORESCENT CLOTHING COLORS

As a digression, let it be said here that whitetail, and apparently all other game animals, are so colorblind as not to be able to distinguish red as such. However, fluorescent colorings apparently reflect light in a fashion so different as to attract attention from both game and man. And either black or white, both uncommon hues in the deer woods and white, well-recognized by game animals, as a danger signal, especially among whitetail, will cause a reaction when seen.

But red, or red-and-black, or even yellow, seem to mean nothing to deer so long as the wearer remains motionless. And therein lies the secret of successful standing—remain dead still.

Smoke if you must; the drift from the pipe or cigarette is helpful to your own judgment of wind movement and is far less disturbing to deer than the hand movements normal to smoking.

HOW TO HUNT IN PAIRS

Hunters who work in two's or three's often use variations of the quiet drive system. For example, if tracks lead into a swamp or a small acreage of heavy cover, two riflemen might circle it quietly, well out, while only one goes through. Or if the area to be hunted is a ridge top, one hunter should work slowly along either side, 200 yards or more down, while the best climber moves along the crest.

If there is a tracking snow and two hunters run onto a trace in which large and deep imprints, plus the toe-drag so common with heavy bucks, indicate a possible whopper ahead, they should not stay together on the trail. One should work along well to the side, 30 to 100 yards out depending on the cover density. The other should stay, not directly in the tracks, but a shade off them to the other side. When, or if, that buck is aware of being followed, or even as a precaution, he will button-hook, or turn perhaps a half circle in order to watch his back trail. Then the wing hunter gets his shot.

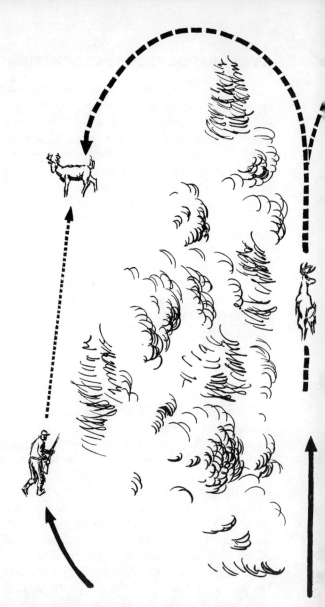

Two or more hunters tracking a heavy buck through snow should work along parallel paths, about 30 to 100 yards to either side, because of the deer habit of button-hooking to protect his back trail

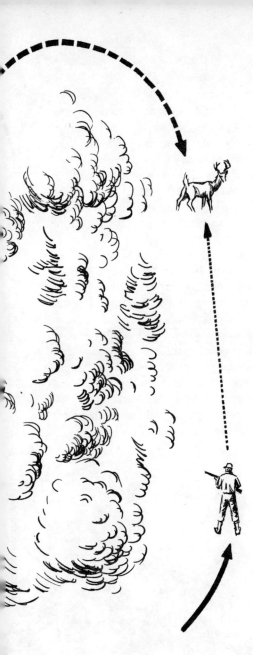

STOP, LOOK, AND LISTEN

Of course, the greatest personal satisfaction comes to the man who hunts alone, who pussyfoots through deer country and nails his buck before the deer spots him. So, far from being a noisy blunderer, this Nimrod moves in tense silence, and above all he moves slowly. He steps not on rustling leaves or snapping sticks but on bare ground or rock; he never climbs onto anything he can step over. He moves only three or four paces before stopping again to look, and to look again, behind as well as ahead or to the side. He remembers that deer may be lying down and, in any event, do not stand a yard high in the timber. So the seasoned hunter looks low, looks not for whole deer but for the flick of ear or tail, the sapling that is not a sapling but a foreleg, the vague shape through brush.

The lone hunter who can figure out where a buck should be bedded—just over the nose of a ridge point from which he can see in several directions, over which flows every revealing current of air, and from which the buck can ease off by the best of several escape routes—and then approach that buck into shooting range, will be the happiest and the most skillful whitetail hunter of all.

BLACKTAILS RESPOND TO CALLS

There are other techniques, most of them local. Over much of his range in the northwestern states and Southeastern Alaska, the small Sitka blacktail, though actually a relative of the mule deer, lives and acts much like the whitetail.

He can be, and is, hunted the same way, with one addition. Whereas whitetail are most irregular in their reaction to a call, especially a call inexpertly used, the little blacktail loves it. Counterfeit correctly the blat of a frightened or hurt fawn and even the bucks move close in curiosity.

By the same token, while tree-sitting is seldom used in the northern states, in Texas the tower, or high-sit, works like a charm in spotting deer drifting through mesquite-high brush. And whereas rattling horns in the cold country, even during rut, has no reputation for productivity, in the Southwest these noises of breeding battle can be a great attraction for some buck which may be within earshot. Probably no game animal is hunted by such a variety of techniques or by methods so directly connected with the local cover as is the whitetail.

41

CHAPTER 4

How to Hunt the Big Mule Deer

Any group of big game hunters sitting around a camp fire can be diverted almost instantly from telling the usual hunting lies into a red-hot argument as to whether the whitetail or the mule deer is the animal harder to hunt. To the devout whitetail fan, old bigears is a dumb ox. He is, they say, wholly without the alertness and the sneaky ability to hide in cover so often demonstrated by the round-eared bucks that happily dwell in eastern areas far less heavily populated than the Rocky Mountain states that comprise mule deer country.

The serious muley hunter, on the other hand, stoutly champions the long-range shooting so often necessary for our western deer, and brags of the ability of tall-horned bucks to disappear on sage flats that will hardly hide a prairie dog. This hassle has been going on for a hundred years. It will cease only when both types of deer become extinct!

MULE DEER DEPENDS ON VISION

There is little doubt that the whitetail is somewhat sneakier in habit, but this is as much a reflection of the relatively dense cover he inhabits and of his experience in living close to mankind, as it is of any ingrained smartness. But the mule deer is no dope, as will be testified by hunters who have consistently hunted them not in open sage country but in Colorado oak thickets or in heavy aspen stands where the long-eared bucks develop a whitetail approach to life.

There are differences in the use of senses. The Virginia

deer relies more on sound as a danger warning than does the muley, for all the difference in ear shape. Since in his normal cover vision is restricted to rather short distances, the Virginia deer places great reliance on scent and sound. The mule deer, particularly when he lives year around in fairly open terrain, or has been driven down onto the semi-desert sage flats by the heavy snows and bitter cold of very late fall, has far greater use of and reliance on his power of sight. It is very likely this reliance on eyesight that leads a buck mule deer, when he has very nearly escaped at his typical bouncing rubber ball gait, to pause just on or near the final skyline for one last look back. That look may well earn him a fatal bullet. It has done much to earn the mule deer his reputation for a low-gear intellect.

MULEYS ARE HIGH ALTITUDE GAME

During the summer months, and until the deep snows come, a high percentage of mule deer live at or above timberline. In Colorado, for example, they range up into bighorn sheep country, as high as 13,000 feet. In most of

One reason mule deer may seem hard to find in open western country is that muleys rely on concealment and can hide behind a tree or clump of sagebrush within a few yards of a hunter, then sneak away

the mule deer states that have high mountain ranges—which is to say most of them—early-season hunts often mean moving far back with pack trains and using a combination of sure-footed mountain horses and equally sure human feet to move around the muley area.

This early hunting, especially for the big timberline bucks, may then resolve itself into a combination of climbing and use of binoculars and spotting scopes to cover the country and pick out a buck from some shady lie up under a cliff. Many a sheep-hunter has inadvertently loosened a rock, watched it bounce, and seen a summer-fat buck bounce off as a result.

SOME LIVE IN LOWLANDS

But there are also mule deer that are year-round residents of the lower country, in the breaks and washes along rivers and coulees, out in the near-desert among the antelope. Actually, until the onrush of winter the mule deer can be found at every elevation from desert to glacier—and can be hunted in as wide a variety of ways.

In this decade, as more and more foothill terrain has been opened up to four-wheel drive vehicles by seismograph and mineral exploration, and as ranchers use fewer horses and more pickups, so have fewer horses been available for hunting. And the classic mule deer hunt involving riding the high mountain parks and exploring canyons on horseback, pausing to glass the country frequently, has fallen less and less into use. More and more mule deer hunters probe into deer country in vehicles, specialized motor-bikes, even tracked snow buggies over late-season snow.

Mule deer may slowly become more gasoline engine-conscious, but today they still tend to stand and look, apparently more curious than frightened by the second-gear grinding of an oncoming vehicle, at ranges easily possible for a rifleman lying steady across the hood of a pickup. This is particularly true in areas that are not hard-hunted.

Mule deer gets reputation for lack of intelligence because he will stop to look back at hunters as he nears the edge of a ridge while making getaway. Wise hunter will have rifle ready to pick him off

Widely practiced and productive of a lot of shooting, such vehicular hunting may run smack into the law in many states. And it is actually more deer *shooting* than it is deer *hunting*.

There comes a time, however, no matter whether the mule deer hunter prefers to travel on a horse or in a go-most-anywhere sort of vehicle, when he has to move afoot.

WORK CANYON SIDES

Save under the peculiar feeding conditions of an extremely late season with bitter cold and 20 or more inches of snow—even big bucks won't stiff it out in deeper snow for long—mule deer use brushy areas, as do whitetail, and gullies and breaks in the terrain as well. The open flats and parks may serve as night feeding areas, but coulees, river breaks, and canyon sides are preferred as day-time bedding spots.

One of the most effective schemes for routing out mule deer with two or three hunters, therefore, is for one man to drop off into the bottom of the coulee or canyon and slowly work his way up the ravine. His companions pace him along the edges or just below the topmost roll of ground.

They should generally try to stay 40 to 50 or even as much as 200 yards ahead, since any buck he chases out of the brushy bottom will probably slant up-canyon in escaping. And they should avoid skylining themselves too frequently, since old bucks will watch those edges and have no intention of jumping into a hunter's lap.

By this scheme, shots may be possible for either hunter, the vision of the buck usually being clearest from the side opposite the slope he climbs, so the gamble of risky long distance shooting can be avoided by picking a narrow canyon. An old muley's lie-up does not require much acreage.

Binoculars or other glassware can be very helpful in locating mule deer. A solid hour spent sitting in one spot in mule deer country usually is far more productive than the same hour used in hiking through the area

In recent years, more foothill terrain has been opened up to four-wheel drive vehicles and fewer horses have been available for hunters. Mule deer are more curious than frightend by appearance of gasoline-powered buggies, making them easy, but illegal, targets for hunters who shoot from vehicles

SHOOT WHEN HE STOPS

Of one thing you can be sure. The escaping mule deer is not going to charge blindly and fast up the far slope. Somewhere before he crests the edge, he will pause, even stand. Sit down and get your rifle ready. That's the time to shoot. It is far wiser to give the deer an added 50 yards of range in exchange for the problems of a running shot.

A similar scheme works handsomely along gullied river breaks, like those along the Missouri above the Fort Peck, Montana, Reservoir. With three hunters in the party, let the man not ambitious to climb work along the base of the steep slopes. Another man patrols the crest; the most ambitious hunter periodically drops part way down to stir up deer hiding in the brushy ravines or to move bucks that may be sunning themselves on a point. With only two men, drop off the low man since the breaks deer usually will run along and up the slopes rather than making for the river.

47

MULEY MAY OUTMANEUVER YOU

Any driving or pushing of mule deer must be planned on a larger scale than for whitetail. The areas will be bigger, more open. This does not mean that mule deer bedded in a choice piece of tall sage or a clump of mountain mahogany will not lie close, relying on concealment. They will. Through binoculars I have watched hatrack bucks lying flat and still as mice while a hunter moved past them at a steady pace. The buck would then either sneak away after the man had passed, or bust out into bouncing flight when the hunter stopped or hesitated, or happened to change course in their direction and so created unbearable tension.

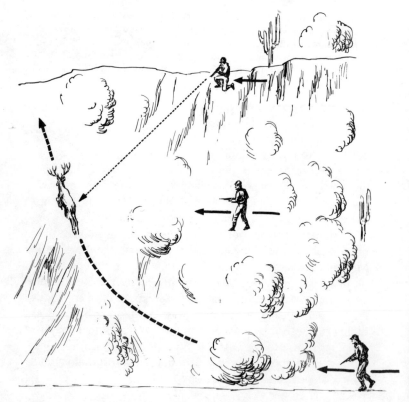

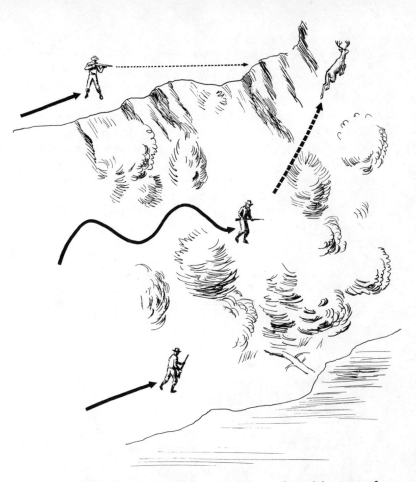

Along gullied river breaks, mule deer are hunted by team of
three. One man works base of steep slopes, second patrols the
crest. The third man drops part way down periodically to stir
up deer in brush

One effective way of routing a mule deer when two or three
hunters are available is to let one man drop off into bottom of
canyon and slowly work his way back up. Other hunters should
stay even with first hunter or just ahead to bag deer which will
run toward top of ravine

As a general rule, however, not as many pushers are needed for mule deer as for whitetail, again a reflection of the difference in the terrain common to the mountain foothills.

On a certain mesa-like formation in northwestern Colorado is a piece of range inhabited by mule deer both through the summer and, particularly, during the late-season migrations. It is not much hunted by the hordes of non-resident hunters because they can't get into it without grave troubles. In daytime, the deer tend to bunch on the brushy benches that drop in a series of steps from the flattened mesa top down to a fair-sized river. Only the does stay up in the sagebrush.

Another adaptation of mule deer driving technique can be used on brushy benches of western terrain. Two men work along topmost rim of mesa while third moves diagonally up and down several benches, stirring up deer in brush. (drawing is not to scale)

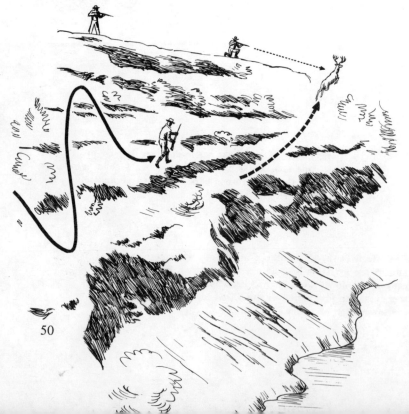

POCKET-SIZE BINOCULARS HELPFUL

Yet one man, sweating diagonally up and down along two or three of these benches, occasionally pausing to roll a rock into any good-looking gully below, was enough to move a considerable number of deer. None of the deer spooked straight for the river. Some fled straight along whatever bench the man was working and disappeared. The majority broke up-hill through two major dry stream beds that notched the benches. They passed within shooting range of the two hunters posted—but kept carefully out of sight —on the topmost rim. To have covered the same amount of whitetail acreage would have called for a small army of drivers and standers.

Far more than with whitetail, though small pocketsize binoculars are often handy in their terrain, good binoculars are the mule deer hunter's best friend. There is so much country to search for big-eared bucks, so many park edges or brush patches to examine for the revealing black nose or sun-glint off antlers that any hunter's eye is helped by 6, 7, 8, or even 9 magnifications.

As with whitetail, a solid hour spent sitting in one spot in mule deer country, using glasses the while, is far more productive than the same hour spent galloping over the countryside.

In the open country of the mule deer, binoculars are handy because there is so much terrain to search for the glint of sun on antlers. Any hunter's eye is helped by 6 to 9 magnifications even with pocket-size glasses

CAREFUL STRATEGY NETS BUCK

Where with whitetail a stalk is an intimate sort of action, all taking place within a half-mile or less, the taking of a big mule deer buck may involve strategy on a grand scale. For example, in Colorado some years back we located with binoculars, and evaluated with a 20X spotting scope, a buck of majestic trophy proportions. He was bedding down with a group of does, half of them casually feeding, some two-thirds of the way up the west-facing slope of a small conical mountain, in a piñon-studded area. Since a steep-sided canyon cut between us and the far mountain, the travel time into the buck's area would be at least an hour, perhaps more.

The shorter and more direct way would bring us onto the slope below the buck. But as that western slope warmed under the afternoon sun, any air currents would drift upward, just as they would, conversely, have tended to drift down the hill while it was in shade. Hence the wiser approach was the longer one, from the back side of the mountain, even though that meant gambling that the deer would stay put until late afternoon. They did, and the shot could be taken from the rocky summit out-cropping.

That the big buck has long since been eaten and his wide-beamed antlers now hang in display was the result of a planned campaign, accounting for all factors of terrain, cover, and wind and involving almost two miles of circuitous travel. Many bucks must be taken that way in mule deer country.

DEER STAY NEAR FOOD SUPPLY

Unless they are being forced into new locations by weather factors such as the snows of late fall, mule deer like whitetail are creatures of habit. They tend to stay within an area offering good feed and water. And when accompanied by a harem of does, as during the rutting season, their movements are even more restricted.

A buck spotted on Tuesday will in all probability be within a mile of that position on Monday next.

In the Sheep Creek area of western Montana, for example, while packing back into the Bitterroots for elk, we located three good breeding bucks. Being interested chiefly in elk we paid them no heed. On the way out 10 days later, by leaving the meat-laden pack train for side-trips, we located two of the three bucks and killed them, each within a half-mile of his earlier hangout.

The old debate as to whether the whitetail or the mule deer is the smarter game animal is a great time-passer, but little more than that. Suffice it to say that the two basic type of North American deer are different, each a challenge in his own way, and where trophy bucks are concerned, each presents a challenge worthwhile to any hunter.

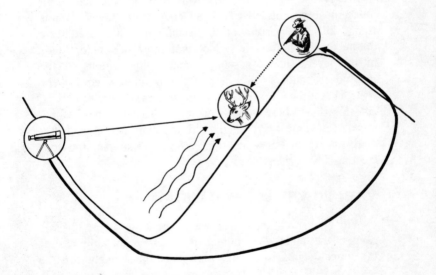

Careful, long-range strategy sometimes pays off in mule deer hunting. Author describes how buck spotted with 20X spotting scope was bagged by taking circuitous route around back side of mountain to avoid air currents drifting upward toward deer on the sunny side of the hill

CHAPTER 5

Mule Deer Rifles and Cartridges

Rifle and cartridge choices for most mule deer hunters are a different matter than for whitetail. Since the big-eared bucks are as a general rule hunted in more open terrain, with the range averaging something like 130 yards and in a surprising percentage of cases stretching farther than that to 200, 300, or possibly more, the demands on rifle and cartridge are different.

The typical mule deer rifle will have a bolt action. In a recent survey of FIELD & STREAM Big Game Honor Badge kills, 70 percent of the identifiable rifles used were of the turning-bolt variety. Not that there are major faults in the lever, slide, or semiautomatic rifle actions in the mule deer calibers. But most western hunters go for the bolt. They probably feel it is more accurate, as it usually is, rifle for rifle. There is no need, or at least less need, for a lot of fast repeat shooting. And the bolt action is better adapted to optical sights than are, for example, the top-ejecting lever rifles.

VARI-POWER SCOPE GAINING

With the premium on precise shooting at pretty fair ranges, the mule deer hunter is almost inevitably a user of optical sights. And his preference is strongly for the 4X glass, though in today's usage the vari-power style of scope, capable of being changed in magnification from 2½X to 7X or 3X to 9X, has gained a lot of adherents. Only about 10 percent of modern mule deer hunters stick to iron sights and they're a diminishing breed.

As was remarked earlier, those muley hunters who go

for scopes of 6X or 8X are usually specialists, fully aware that they are sacrificing the field of view needed for running shots in order to get high definition at long range. A mule deer fan can hardly go wrong in using a 4X of as good quality as his pocketbook can handle.

Much the same lines of reasoning have developed the proper preferences in cartridges for mule deer use. The shot can be anticipated at anywhere from 100 to 350 yards —beyond that any shooting is chancy even for a skilled rifleman and to cover so much range difference means a cartridge in the upper velocity brackets, say above 2,500 feet per second at the rifle muzzle. The round must shoot flat; its bullet must hold enough speed and energy at range to do an honest and sportsmanlike job of deer-slaying halfway across a sizeable sagebrush flat.

Some mule deer hunters prefer bolt action rifles because they feel they're more accurate at long ranges and it's easier to mount optical sights on a rifle that does not eject empty shells through the top. They are also available in a variety of chamberings

55

A bullet's trajectory will carry the slug several inches above the line of sight, after which it will gradually drop toward the ground as it moves away from the rifle muzzle. Using the Rule of Three, a hunter can determine at what range the bullet will cross the line of sight, where it will be three inches below, and 12 inches below. See page 122

LONG SHOT NEEDED FOR MULEY

For this reason, even the trusty old .30-30 is slowly going out of use save among those who hunt muleys as we hunt whitetail, by prowling the oak brush and aspen stands. The same might be said for the .35 Remington, the .348 and a host of other cartridges, largely in the under-2,500 class, not that they will not handle muleys within their proper range, because they will, but rather because they fall down on those long tries. At 300 yards, for example, the .30-30 hits with only half the wallop of a .30-06 load, and hitting the vital area with it at such yardage is a problem in ballistic guesswork beyond any but the luckiest or the most expert.

The same survey, made in 1963, listed the top choices in order as: .30-06, .270 Winchester, .30-30 and .308 Winchester, .300 Savage, .264 Winchester Magnum, .243 Winchester, .257 Roberts, 8 mm. Mauser. Sharing the 10th spot were the .303 British, .280 Remington, and .300 Holland & Holland.

If we were to update the survey to accommodate the kills that will be made this fall, however, it is reasonable that the top 10 makeup would be changed slightly since there are new cartridges that have caught the hunter's fancy. The 7 mm. Remington Magnum would be one outstanding addition. The .300 Winchester Magnum would be another, and it is likely that the 6 mm. Remington would have won its fair share of adherents. The .358 Winchester and .338 Winchester Magnum would have won some friends, and so eventually will the 6.5 Remington Magnum now becoming available.

OLDER CARTRIDGES ON DECLINE

Precisely how they'll all rank is hard to say, but reason and long experience indicate that the old and the slow will drop further down on the preference list, the trend will continue toward the more modern high velocity items, less because they are more deadly on deer, though they generally are, than because they are easier to hit with regardless of range. Of one point we can be certain—not readily will the .30-06 and the .270 relinquish their leading positions—simply because there are so many rifles in these calibers.

Essentially, then, what the mule deer hunter prefers—and properly so—is a cartridge that develops some 1,400 foot-pounds of striking force at 200 yards, or over 1,000 foot-pounds at 300. And he prefers his killing wallop to be on the high side of those figures. He also properly wants a combination such that, when the scope-sighted rifle is targeted so that bullets impact three inches above point of aim at 100 yards, the bullet path will curve back down through the line of sight not before the 200 yard point or mighty close to it.

In short, he wants a cartridge which, when the Rule of Three is applied in the original sighting-in, will let him hold point blank on the deer's shoulder out to anywhere between 225 and 325 yards, depending on the original velocity and the ability, the weight and shape factors, of the bullet to hold its speed, and still expect to strike within a six-inch circle. As a rough rule of thumb, this means cartridges using bullets of 100 grains weight or more and developing muzzle velocities of over 2,500 feet per second.

IF RECOIL IS A PROBLEM

Where recoil is a serious consideration, as it often is for the ladies and for beginning riflemen, the mule deer hunter will find that cartridges on the order of the .243 Winchester, the 6 mm. Remington, the .257 Roberts, the 7 mm. Mauser, and probably the new 6.5 Remington Magnum, will handle deer without hurting the shooter's shoulder. For the run-of-the-mill hunter who is not seriously bothered by recoil and also plans on occasion to use his rifle on other western game like elk, goat, bear, and so on, the cartridges in the class of the .270 Winchester, .280 Remington, .308 and .30-06, the 8 mm. Mauser with proper loadings, will do the job well enough.

If recoil is no problem and the hunter wants the ability to stretch for those long-range kills, the assorted magnums like the Weatherby series, then the .264 and .300 Winchester types, the 7 mm. Magnum in either the Remington case form or one of its competitors among the wildcats or the less-known 7 x 61, are just the ticket. They do, as a general rule, develop significantly flatter trajectories and carry, as

The body structure of a deer is such that the bullet used should penetrate about six inches before full expansion. A bullet that expands on impact or cuts through the body without expanding may not kill the deer quickly or at all, allowing a wounded animal to escape

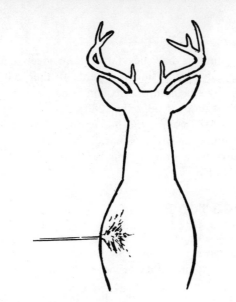

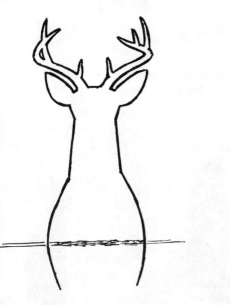

you can see from the ballistics tables, any given caliber's level of energy at least a hundred yards further out. The 7 mm. Weatherby Magnum, for example, has at 300 yards about as much wallop as does the .280 Remington at 200. For such bonuses of course the hunter must pay in added recoil, muzzle noise, and rate of barrel wear. But in today's competitive hunting, a growing number figure the Magnum is worth such costs.

SOME SLUGS TOO BIG

The mule deer hunter hardly needs, of course, any of the large-caliber sluggers like the .338 Winchester or the .375 Holland & Holland, since they're meant for beasts weighing considerably more than the average deer.

Most experienced deer hunters select the medium weight of bullet in any given caliber. That would mean the 130-grain for the .270 Winchester, as one example, or the 150-grain .30-06 loading, or the 140 to 160 weight levels in any .28 caliber or 7 mm.

Their reasoning is simple enough. First, it does not re-

Recommended bullets for deer hunting should be soft points with a good exposure of lead, peg points, some in the hollow point category, as well as two-core slugs

quire a slug of 200 or more grains to drop any deer, not even a fat muley. In fact, the nervous system, musculature and bone structure of deer are such that they usually drop more quickly to a bullet of high velocity at impact than to a slower, if heavier, projectile. Second, the medium-weight bullet usually balances off weight, diameter, and point shape to retain its speed, so hit harder and shoot flatter, than either the short-bodied lightweight or the longer but slower-starting bullet in any given caliber.

MOST HOLLOW-POINT SLUGS O.K.

Further, the body structure of a deer, even a muley, is seldom so massive that a bullet of really slow expansion or extra-penetration power is needed. The bullet which is designed to expand or break up immediately on impact, the very lightweight varmint bullet, is of course too frangible. But for deer, a projectile rating on the fast-to-medium expansion rate, one that will deliver its energy in a single numbing punch, seems to offer peak killing surety because of the deer's sensitivity to what has been called hydrostatic shock.

Without regard to technicalities, then, the body mass of a deer is such that a bullet capable of penetrating roughly six inches before full expansion is quite adequate. Therefore,

most soft points with good exposure of lead, most hollow points, peg points, protected hollow points and capped points will fill the bill. Bullets of the two-core variety, while originally meant for heavier game, also work well on deer.

As for the whitetail hunter, faith in a rifle and cartridge, belief born of experience, is half the battle in killing cleanly. This is particularly true in the wide-open spaces where hitting the chest area of a buck may not be so much a matter of paper ballistics as it is of knowledge of the rifle and cartridge, and practice with them, so that their in-built characteristics are effectively used.

All the fulminations of the arms writers, interesting though they be, pale into insignificance when confronted with one hard fact of hunting—"It aint what you hit 'em with, it's where you hit 'em that counts."

CHAPTER 6

Rifles and Cartridges for Whitetail

Lock 10 serious whitetail hunters into a cabin for two days and you'll have a minor riot on your hands. The first day they'll argue about rifles and cartridges for whitetail in amicable fashion, with nobody really red-eared, but by nightfall one will be sore that his .45-70 isn't thought much by the high-velocity fans. By noon of the second day the .270 Winchester fancier will be waving a clenched fist under the snoot of a .35 Remington adherent. The amazing part of it all is that such high blood pressure really isn't necessary. Come right down to it, the good whitetail rifle is the one you take whitetail bucks with.

A few years ago, from the thousands of application blanks for FIELD & STREAM Big Game Honor Badges, whitetail category, we pulled 500 at random and worked out the statistics as to rifle models actually used, calibers, sights, number of shots required, even range. That the range averaged out at 65 yards was no surprise. That has been the average on whitetail for decades and probably never will be changed much.

That buckshot and particularly rifled slugs ranked as high in cartridge choice as 4th and 3rd was definitely jarring. That the .30-06 rated first in cartridges and the .30-30 second, on the other hand, merited no comment at all. The .30-06 was for over 50 years our official military cartridge so there are countless numbers of rifles for it. And the .30-30 has since 1894 probably killed more North American game animals than any other centerfire round.

Lever action rifles offer versatility of speed for repeat firing, light weight, especially in carbines, and adaptability to use of scopes

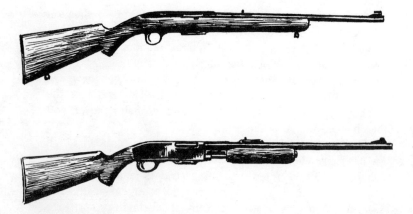

Whitetail hunters may like the semi-automatic or pump action rifle which permits quick firing or repeat shooting at rather close range

BUCKSHOT RANGE LIMITED

Before we go into the specifics of whitetail rifles and cartridges for them, let's take care of shotgun matters. Buckshot, though widely used—even required by law in some southern states and in certain counties of the northern deer states—can hardly be considered the most reliable deer-slayer. Recent loadings using plastic shot holders, with the pellets of buckshot placed in polyethylene chips to lessen the flattening of the shot in their passage down the gun barrel—in order to help them fly true—have helped matters. Buckshot of any size is viciously effective out to about 30 yards. Thus, it is enough in really thick country where deer must be driven by hounds or men. But at 50 yards, only five of the nine pellets in a conventional load of 00 size shot will hit the deer anywhere. At 60 yards, he'll be struck by only two or three and those will punch vital spots only by sheer chance.

The effective range of buckshot then is severely limited. The basic rule of thumb is to use a full choke gun unless you happen on one that patterns the large pellets uniquely well, and to try to hold your fire beyond 40 paces.

SMALL SLUGS LACK KILLING POWER

The rifled slug and an open-bored shotgun equipped with sights—and every manufacturer has such in his line—has enough more to be said for it, however, to be called the poor man's deer rifle. From such a sight-equipped gun, modern slugs will stay within a three to four inch group at 50 yards. That is little worse than some rifles and is amply accurate for thick-country hunting.

The umbrella-shaped blob of lead, almost three-fourths of an inch across and expanding further on impact, makes a large and deadly wound, even though the energy factor for the 12-gauge one-ounce slug is down to 1,300 foot-pounds by the 50-step mark.

At 100 yards, the slug cluster is likely to spread well be-

DEER CARTRIDGES

* Based on factory-released figures for cartridges most used in U. S. For data on other imported or independently loaded calibers consult importer or manufacturer. Free tables listing all bullet types and loads available can be obtained from sales or shooting promotion divisions of major companies. Riflemen are reminded that ballistics is an inexact science, that impossibility of control of individual barrel, load, firing conditions, renders all figures meaningful only as reasonably close approximations.

CARTRIDGE	BULLET Wt. Grs.	VELOCITY Ft. Per. Sec.				ENERGY Ft. Lbs.				MID-RANGE Trajectory		
		Muzzle	100 yds.	200 yds.	300 yds.	Muzzle	100 yds.	200 yds.	300 yds.	100 yds.	200 yds.	300 yds.
243 Winchester	80	3500	3080	2720	2410	2280	1690	1320	1030	0.4	1.8	4.7
243 Winchester	100	3070	2790	2540	2320	2090	1730	1430	1190	0.5	2.2	5.5
244 Remington	75	3500	3070	2660	2290	2040	1570	1180	875	0.4	1.9	4.9
244 Remington	90	3200	2850	2530	2230	2050	1630	1280	995	0.5	2.1	5.5
6 m/m Remington	100	3190	2920	2660	2420	2260	1890	1570	1300	0.5	2.1	5.1
25 Remington	117	2320	1980	1700	1470	1400	1020	750	560	1.0	4.5	11.5
25-35 Winchester	117	2300	1910	1600	1340	1370	945	665	465	1.0	4.6	12.5
250 Savage	87	3030	2660	2330	2060	1770	1370	1050	820	0.6	2.5	6.4
250 Savage	100	2820	2460	2140	1870	1760	1340	1020	775	0.6	2.9	7.4
256 Winchester Magnum	60	2800	2070	1570	1220	1040	570	330	200	0.8	4.0	12.0
257 Roberts	100	2900	2540	2210	1920	1870	1430	1080	820	0.6	2.7	7.0
257 Roberts	117	2650	2280	1950	1690	1820	1350	985	740	0.7	3.4	8.8
257 Weatherby Magnum	87	3825	3290	2835	2450	2828	2087	1553	1160	0.3	1.6	4.4
257 Weatherby Magnum	100	3555	3150	2815	2500	2802	2199	1760	1388	0.4	1.7	4.4
257 Weatherby Magnum	117	3300	2900	2550	2250	2824	2184	1689	1315	0.4	2.4	6.8
264 Winchester Magnum	100	3700	3260	2880	2550	3040	2360	1840	1440	0.4	1.6	4.2

Cartridge	Grains											
264 Winchester Magnum	140	3200	2940	2700	2480	3180	2690	2270	1910	0.5	2.1	4.9
270 Winchester	100	3580	3160	2770	2400	2840	2210	1700	1280	0.4	1.7	4.5
270 Winchester	130	3140	2850	2580	2320	2840	2340	1920	1550	0.5	2.1	5.3
270 Winchester	150	2800	2400	2040	1750	2610	1920	1380	1020	0.7	3.0	7.8
270 Weatherby Magnum	100	3760	3265	2825	2435	3140	2363	1772	1317	0.4	1.6	4.3
270 Weatherby Magnum	130	3375	3050	2750	2480	3283	2686	2183	1776	0.4	1.8	4.5
270 Weatherby Magnum	150	3245	2955	2675	2430	3501	2909	2385	1967	0.5	2.0	5.0
7x57 m/m Mauser	175	2490	2170	1900	1680	2410	1830	1400	1100	0.8	3.7	9.5
280 Remington	100	3570	3160	2770	2420	2830	2220	1700	1300	0.4	1.8	4.5
280 Remington	125	3190	2880	2590	2320	2820	2300	1860	1490	0.5	2.1	5.3
280 Remington	150	2890	2660	2440	2210	2780	2360	1980	1630	0.6	2.5	6.1
280 Remington	165	2820	2510	2220	1970	2910	2310	1810	1420	0.6	2.8	7.2
284 Winchester	125	3200	2880	2590	2310	2840	2300	1860	1480	0.5	2.1	5.3
284 Winchester	150	2900	2630	2380	2160	2800	2300	1890	1550	0.6	2.5	6.3
7x61 S&H	160	3100	2927	2757	2595	3010	3040	2700	2385	0.1	1.5	4.3
7 m/m Remington Magnum	150	3260	2970	2700	2450	3540	2940	2430	1930	0.4	2.0	4.9
7 m/m Remington Magnum	175	3070	2860	2660	2460	3660	3170	2740	2350	0.5	2.1	5.2
7 m/m Weatherby Magnum	139	3300	2995	2715	2465	3355	2770	2275	1877	0.4	1.9	4.9
7 m/m Weatherby Magnum	154	3160	2885	2640	2415	3406	2847	2384	1994	0.5	2.0	5.0
30 Carbine	110	1980	1540	1230	1040	950	575	370	260	1.4	7.5	21.7
30-30 Winchester	150	2410	2020	1700	1430	1930	1360	960	680	0.9	4.2	11.0
30-30 Winchester	170	2220	1890	1630	1410	1860	1350	1000	750	1.2	4.6	12.5
30 Remington	170	2220	1890	1630	1410	1860	1350	1000	750	1.2	4.6	12.5
30-40 Krag	180	2470	2120	1830	1590	2440	1790	1340	1010	0.8	3.8	9.9
30-40 Krag	220	2200	1990	1800	1630	2360	1930	1580	1300	1.0	4.4	11.0
308 Winchester	110	3340	2810	2340	1920	2730	1930	1340	900	0.5	2.2	6.0
308 Winchester	150	2860	2570	2300	2050	2730	2200	1760	1400	0.6	2.6	6.5
308 Winchester	180	2610	2390	2170	1970	2720	2280	1870	1540	0.8	3.1	7.4
308 Winchester	200	2450	2210	1980	1770	2670	2170	1750	1400	0.8	3.6	9.0
30-06 Springfield	110	3420	2880	2400	1970	2850	2020	1410	945	0.4	2.1	5.6

DEER CARTRIDGES

CARTRIDGE	BULLET Wt. Grs.	VELOCITY Ft. Per. Sec. Muzzle	100 yds.	200 yds.	300 yds.	ENERGY Ft. Lbs. Muzzle	100 yds.	200 yds.	300 yds.	MID-RANGE Trajectory 100 yds.	200 yds.	300 yds.
30-06 Springfield	150	2970	2670	2400	2130	2930	2370	1920	1510	0.6	2.4	6.1
30-06 Springfield	180 R.N.	2700	2330	2010	1740	2910	2170	1610	1210	0.7	3.1	8.3
30-06 Springfield	180	2700	2470	2250	2040	2910	2440	2020	1660	0.7	2.9	7.0
30-06 Springfield	220	2410	2120	1870	1670	2830	2190	1710	1360	0.8	3.9	9.8
300 Savage	150	2670	2390	2130	1890	2370	1900	1510	1190	0.7	3.0	7.6
300 Savage	180	2370	2040	1760	1520	2240	1660	1240	920	0.9	4.1	10.5
300 H & H Magnum	180	2920	2670	2440	2220	3400	2850	2380	1970	0.6	2.4	5.8
300 H & H Magnum	220	2620	2370	2150	1940	3350	2740	2260	1840	0.7	3.1	7.7
300 Winchester Magnum	150	3400	3050	2730	2430	3850	3100	2480	1970	0.4	1.9	4.8
300 Winchester Magnum	180	3070	2850	2640	2440	3770	3250	2790	2380	0.5	2.1	5.3
300 Weatherby Magnum	150	3545	3195	2890	2615	4179	3393	2783	2279	0.4	1.5	3.9
300 Weatherby Magnum	180	3245	2960	2705	2475	4201	3501	2925	2448	0.4	1.9	5.2
300 Weatherby Magnum	220	2905	2610	2385	2150	4123	3329	2757	2257	0.6	2.5	6.7
308 Norma Magnum	180	3100	2881	2668	2464	3842	3318	2846	2427	.0	1.6	4.6
303 Savage	190	1980	1680	1440	1250	1650	1190	875	660	1.3	6.2	15.5
303 British	215	2180	1900	1660	1460	2270	1720	1310	1020	1.1	4.9	12.5
32 Winchester Special	170	2280	1870	1560	1330	1960	1320	920	665	1.0	4.8	13.0
32 Remington	170	2220	1890	1610	1400	1860	1350	975	740	1.0	4.9	13.0
338 Winchester Magnum	200	3000	2690	2410	2170	4000	3210	2580	2090	0.5	2.4	6.0
338 Winchester Magnum	250	2700	2430	2180	1940	4050	3280	2640	2090	0.7	3.0	7.0
348 Winchester	150	2890	2360	1860	1420	2780	1850	1150	670	0.6	3.2	9.0
348 Winchester	200	2530	2140	1820	1570	2840	2030	1470	1090	0.8	3.8	10.0
348 Winchester	250	2350	1970	1660	1410	3060	2150	1530	1100	0.9	4.4	11.5
35 Remington	200	2210	1830	1540	1310	2170	1490	1050	760	1.1	5.2	14.0
350 Remington Magnum	200	2725	2355	2025	1730	3290	2465	1820	1325	0.7	3.2	8.3

Cartridge	Bullet Wt.											
350 Remington Magnum	250	2410	2135	1885	1660	3220	2535	1975	1530	0.8	3.8	9.8
358 Winchester	200	2530	2210	1910	1640	2840	2160	1610	1190	0.8	3.6	9.4
358 Winchester	250	2250	2010	1780	1570	2810	2230	1760	1370	1.0	4.4	11.0
358 Norma Magnum	250	2790	2493	2231	2001	4322	3451	2764	2223	0.2	2.4	6.6
375 H & H Magnum	270	2740	2460	2210	1990	4500	3620	2920	2370	0.7	2.9	7.1
375 H & H Magnum	300	2550	2280	2040	1830	4330	3460	2770	2230	0.7	3.3	8.3
375 Weatherby Magnum	270	2900	2610	2330	2115	5041	4035	3254	2684	0.6	2.5	6.8
375 Weatherby Magnum	300	2750	2490	2230	2015	5037	4131	3312	2706	0.7	2.9	7.0
378 Weatherby Magnum	270	3180	2850	2600	2315	6051	4871	4053	3210	0.5	2.0	5.2
378 Weatherby Magnum	300	2925	2610	2380	2125	5700	4539	3774	3009	0.6	2.5	6.2
401 Winchester Self-Loading	200	2190	1650	1220	1010	2130	1210	660	455	1.2	6.3	19.0
44-40 Winchester	200	1310	1050	940	830	760	490	390	305	3.3	15.0	36.5
44 Magnum	240	1750	1360	1110	980	1630	985	655	510	1.6	8.4	—
45-70 Government	405	1320	1160	1050	990	1570	1210	990	880	2.9	13.0	32.5
458 Winchester Magnum	510 S.P.	2125	1840	1600	1400	5110	3830	2900	2220	1.1	5.1	13.2
458 Winchester Magnum	500 Solid	2125	1910	1700	1520	5010	4050	3210	2570	1.1	4.8	12.0
460 Weatherby Magnum	500	2700	2330	2005	1730	8095	6025	4465	3320	0.7	3.3	10.0

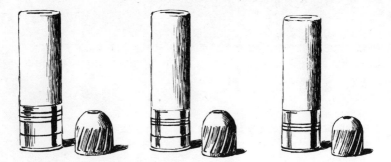

The shotgun, open-bored and equipped with sights, has been called the poor man's deer rifle. It can be used to fire rifled slugs like those shown in the illustration although accuracy may be lost at ranges beyond 60 to 70 yards; killing energy is lacking in small gauge slugs

yond a foot. So common sense indicates that with slugs the true sportsman will hold his shot at any buck beyond 60 or at most 70 yards. If he's smart, he'll avoid for slug use: (1) double-barrels, which tend to crossfire; (2) tight-bored guns, which help accuracy not at all though the slugs won't hurt the choke; or, (3) smoothbores without sights because lacking sights he won't really know where his chunk of lead is going. And he'll also forget slugs in any gauge smaller than 20, since the .410-gauge slug of only one-fifth ounce weight hasn't killing energies surely adequate for deer even at the gun muzzle.

HUNTER USUALLY CLOSE TO WHITETAIL

Practical though it is in much of the whitetail country, however, the rifled slug has little of the appeal of those centerfire rifle cartridges which will start disagreements among whitetail hunters. But if we look at the matter logically, perhaps we can reduce the choice of rifles and cartridges to reasonable limits. Perhaps.

First off, the whitetail hunter's shot may come at ranges

measuring from a few feet to about 150 yards. Rarely are his chances longer. Exceptions occur among the road-hunters in some states who patrol the byways until they see deer feeding high in the pasture, or among those devotees of the extreme-range try who pot deer with special equipment at from 600 to 1000 yards.

His average shot, therefore, need be no marvel of precision. Nor does he need precision but rather speed of handling and fire to cope with a buck that has already busted loose and is flitting off through the birches. Finally, he will, unless he is a confirmed stump-sitter, be carrying his rifle at the ready much of the time, and for long hours before he gets a shot at all.

GUN SHOULD BE LIGHT, FAST

Reasonably, therefore, the whitetail hunter prefers a light, short-barreled arm, on the carbine style. He is far more likely to plump for the quick-firing semi-automatic, slide, or lever action rifle—and aimed shots can be gotten off in just about that same order of speed—than he is for the slower-operating but more precise bolt action. Nor is he generally concerned about the ability of his musket to hit a 50-cent piece every time at 200 yards because he simply isn't going to shoot that far.

The writer does most of his own whitetail hunting with a small-caliber wildcat rifle, a .240 P.S.P. with a 4X scope and about 3,200 foot-seconds of muzzle velocity. But unlike most deer hunters, he rarely bothers fast-running game and he does much of his whitetail hunting sitting down or standing still. The general run of whitetail fan is happiest, however, with a quick-firing rifle weighing as much under eight pounds as he can find, preferably around seven pounds.

LOW POWER SCOPES HELPFUL

By the same token—the factors of short range and running targets—many deer hunters still tend to uphold the

71

virtues of open sights, though the smarter ones have shifted to the more efficient peep and the smart older ones have long since gone to optical sights. Scopes in the 1X to 3X and at most 4X categories are the general choice. A broad field of view, and plenty of light-gathering power for those late November afternoons, they correctly figure, are needed.

Deer hunters further rarely use the rifle sling, or even the carrying strap, figuring to have Old Betsy ready for instant use. But here again, some of the smarter ones have discovered that the European *jaeger* style of slinging a rifle muzzle down over the left shoulder will, with practice, let a man get his carbine into action as fast as does hand-carrying in any position.

HEAVY BULLETS IN HEAVY BRUSH

Since whitetail deer are hardly—on the average—large animals, no cannon is needed to stop them. At the same time it is true that a frightened whitetail with his heart shot half away often summons enough reserve adrenalin to carry him several hundred yards before he finally drops. The best excuse for large calibers is their brush-bucking ability. There is no getting around the theory that a large, heavy, slow, round-nosed bullet is less likely to be deflected, and almost never broken up, by contact with twigs or branches than is the light, pointed, fast bullet.

Any thinking man must also realize that whether or not his bullet hits the deer behind brush depends more on where the brush is than any other factor. Since bullet deflection

The brain, heart, and lungs are the most vulnerable target areas if they are exposed to the hunter who may have to make a quick decision. The heart is located near the front and bottom of the body cavity (marked by white circle); lungs fill much of the body cavity above the heart. Neck and spine shots also make quick kills

must be angular, clearly if the branch is close to the gun muzzle the shot will be a miss; if it's close enough to the deer there's a good chance for a hit.

However, luck has a way of siding with common sense, so the use of low-velocity items like the .35 Remington, the .30-30, .32 Winchester Special, the .44 S&W Magnum as used in a rifle, the old .45-70, and all the rest of the breed goes on and on, and probably will do so for years to come.

OTHER CARTRIDGE CHOICES

Most whitetail hunters follow much the same reasoning with other cartridges. The .308 Winchester, for example, is a handy round of adequate power for any deer, and all quick-firing types of rifle action are barreled for it. The .30-06 is available in both semiautomatic and pump action muskets. With these as with the older .300 Savage cartridge, the tendency is to plump for the heavier bullets, say the 180-grain round-nosed style, even though many experienced whitetail hunters have come to realize that lighter and faster projectiles drop deer faster.

By and large, save where they're used by men who have other purposes—we might call them western purposes like mule deer, sheep, antelope and such—for their rifles, the modern highspeed cartridges find little favor among confirmed whitetail artists. The .270 Winchester, .280 Remington, the .243 Winchester and 6 mm. Remington, the .257— though many still like it with the 117-grain bullet—and the entire clan of modern magnums are considered by many too fast, too likely of bullet break-up or wild deflection in brushy country. They will of course kill whitetail deer with stunning speed and are, despite the brush factor, quite reasonable choices, except for the big magnums. Little or no reason exists to use on whitetail those rounds developing 3,000 to 4,000 foot-pounds of striking force. They may well destroy the edibility of half the buck, for one thing!

LEGAL LIMITS FOR BULLETS

As left-overs from the past, we today have a large number of cartridges which are marginal in their sporting application to whitetail, items like the .25-20, .32-20, .32-40, .38-40 and .38-55 which are long-lived black powder cartridges now loaded with smokeless powders. We also have the .35 and .351 WSL types, newer but used in actions never meant for high-powered centerfires. Each and every one of these has killed many deer. And in the hands of a properly careful hunter, one who shoots only when he is dead certain of making a clean neck or heart shot, all of them will continue to handle deer.

But as a general rule these oldsters fall short of the minimum bullet-energy requirements set by law in some states—on the order of 1,400 foot-pounds at the muzzle, or in some states an equivalent striking force out at 100 yards —and their continued use cannot be recommended in good conscience.

Much the same could be said of the .30 caliber carbine, now commercially loaded with soft-point bullets. Too few hunters of today are sufficiently skilled to be certain of tracking down any deer they may wound.

NO PERFECT RIFLE & CARTRIDGE

The .22 centerfires, like the .222 Remington and .222 Magnum, the .225 Winchester, .22-250 and .220 Swift class of cartridge, are likewise by most hunters held unsporting for use on deer. Every seasoned hunter has, under the right conditions, accomplished many clean kills. One game warden in an eastern state, charged with herd reduction in a controlled area, dropped 52 deer in succession with the .222, without a single trail-up or failure. But the high speed bullets can hardly be expected to plow through brush, and much of their nearly explosive killing effect is nullified when the rifle is in the hands of the sort of hunter who for reason either of low-skill level or mere excitement fails to place the small bullet perfectly.

The perfect whitetail rifle and cartridge will probably never emerge, not if it has to satisfy every Nimrod who heads for the woods, red-capped or red-coated, in the late fall. This is just as well for the makers of rifles and ammunition. But one point about deer rifles already has emerged: the cartridge and rifle that best suit you, that you can cleanly kill buck whitetail with, are by all odds the best combination for you. If Grandpop likes an octagon-barreled .45-70 and open sights, and you prefer a scoped .243, the chances are you'll both come home with vension, providing you spot your shots correctly.

CHAPTER **7**

Glassware for Deer Hunters

One of the major phenomena during the past two decades of the sporting arms business has been the democratization of the scope sight. Prior to the last great war, optical sights were rarities, known only to specialists, cursed by great cost and disconcerting fragility. But when hostilities ceased, a wave of development and manufacturing effort swept the country to make completely reliable optics and a variety of likewise reliable mounting systems available at prices within the reach of every shooter and hunter. Now the optical hunting sight has come to belong to every Tom, Dick, and Harry—even to the deer hunters.

Classically, the sights on "deer rifles" have been among the least efficient used on any sporting arm. The choice of thousands was for an amazingly long period the buckhorn rear sight, with a fine bead front. The buckhorn itself, often only coarsely adjustable by a stepped elevation slide, with a hammer needed to knock in any windage corrections, had up-swooping side wings or horns that merely served to conceal the game, especially the moving animal for which the design was presumably created. The little notch in the center of the blade, into which the 1/16-inch front bead was theoretically to be pulled for a "fine bead" was itself usually

One of the older, simpler gunsights still in use is the buckhorn or semi-buckhorn with notches for raising or lowering the elevation

so fine that the pulling left time enough for the buck to depart.

MIDDLE-AGE EYESIGHT HAZARDS

Like the buckhorn, the conventional rear sight with which most factory-made rifles are still wastefully equipped poses focusing problems impossible for most men over 45. It is not particularly fast in its usual shape, with a flat bar U-notched in the middle. It does obscure the target and it does take even a reasonably trained man time to consciously pull the front sight bead or blade down to precisely the correct level. It is likewise coarse in adjustment. Probably its best form, rarely seen on factory-supplied rifles as made today, is the type modeled after the express sights found on large-caliber British double rifles, elephant guns, in which the blade top is cut as a very shallow V, and a vertical line of gold or platinum leads up into the base of the V so that rolling a large front bead down into the V center is both fast and instinctive.

For the eyes of all but the young (certainly for the eyes of the middle-aged who are among our most confirmed group of hunters), normal aging or lens-hardening makes it most

difficult, with or without corrective lenses, to bring into simultaneous focus a rear sight 10 to 16 inches from the aiming eye, a front sight 12 to 16 inches farther away than that, and a buck deer standing out at 75 yards. As a result, it is a rare man beyond 40-odd who with open sights can shoot groups better than three or four inches at a hundred yards, even with a rest and ample time.

LESS FOCUS PROBLEM WITH PEEP

The peep sight, old as the hills in target-shooting usage, is one means of dodging the focus problem. Since the human eye normally and inevitably tends to center any object seen through a circular hole, no matter how fuzzy or unfocussed that hole may be, with a peep sight the hunter needs to concern himself about focussing only on his front sight and on the target many yards away. He can forget about bringing the peep itself into focus; can let it fuzz. He should for deer hunting deliberately use one with a coarse peep insert or no insert at all rather than the pinhole types preferred for target shooting. He'll shoot better and in a very short time will be shooting faster, so will become more deadly on game.

Three views of a deer as it would appear through different types of sights. As the hunter gets along in years, it becomes more difficult to line up back sight, front sight, and target in a hurry because the eye loses ability to accommodate. Scope helps solve that problem

The close-mounted peep, easily adjusted with thumb or slotted screws to give both elevation and windage change to known amounts, according either to distinct clicks or similarly clear line markings, is a tremendous improvement over the open sight.

OPTICAL SIGHTS HELP HUNTER

The virtues of the peep seem to have been recognized among the deer-hunting clan rather late in the game. And most seem to jump over it, moving directly from outdated open sights to the optical sight, the scope. Very likely the major reason is that with a hunting telescope there is no problem of focus whatever. The aiming point, be it crosshairs, a dot, a post or some combination, always appears to be pasted against the side of the target object. The hunter just puts it over, or a shade behind, the shoulder of his buck and lets go. It matters not whether his eyes are 20/20 or are equipped with glasses as thick as bottle bottoms. The optical sight also permits seeing the game whole and far more clearly than with the naked eye. It makes identification of buck or doe—or some other hunter—markedly easier. It either contains its own internal adjustment scheme for shifting the aiming point or reticle in windage and elevation or has nearly as simple a method within the mount. Through its light-collecting ability, it extends the hunting day anywhere from 15 minutes to half an hour at either end.

MODERN SIGHTS MORE RUGGED

Years ago the optical sight was a tender instrument, fragile enough to fail under hunting's ordinary knocks, prone to leakage of humid air and so to fogging under temperature change. But these objections have largely disappeared under improvements in design, in lens-mounting cements and in sealing methods. Further, as of today, the rifle-owner has available to him a variety of scope mounts highly reliable in engineering, made to suit virtually any combination of

Peep sights may range from simple to sophisticated but have the advantage of helping the hunter to line up the sight and target quickly. Various knobs permit adjustment for elevation and windage

rifle, scope, and shooting circumstance.

The white tail hunter gets most of his chances at bucks within 100 yards. As a matter of fact, the national average would probably work out close to 65 yards. He may hunt in fairly thick timber, find most deer moving early and late in the short days of latter fall, hence will be operating in rather poor light. He may get a high percentage of moving or even running shots, especially if he moves around much or is a stander on large-scale drives. Logically, then, the rifle scope best suited to his job is one that has a broad field of view, a high level of brilliance or light-gathering ability, and a rather coarse aiming point, one that will retain some visibility after sunset, and is quickly caught by his eye.

HOW TO FIGURE POWER

In broad terms this means that the whitetail hunter does best with a scope with tube and objective lens an inch or more in diameter, a magnification rating of 2X, 2½X, 2-¾X, 3X, or at most 4X. These limitations are set by optical

81

laws. Although 2X is interpreted simply as "two power," the figure is determined by dividing the diameter of the objective lens by the diameter of the exit pupil, a term meaning the area of light concentrated in the center of the eyepiece.

The light efficiency of a scope is rated by its relative brilliance. And you use the same factors of power, objective diameter, and exit pupil to calculate the relative brightness. For example, a scope with an objective lens 19 millimeters in diameter and an exit pupil of 7.6 millimeters would be a 2½ power scope. To get the relative brilliance, you square the figure for the exit pupil, or multiply 7.6 by 7.6, and obtain a rating of approximately 58.

By comparison, the same objective lens with a power of 6X would have an exit pupil of only 3.2 (19 divided by 6) and the relative brilliance rating would be 10 (3.2 multiplied by 3.2). In other words, power is not the only factor to consider because a small-lensed 6X scope could be dim indeed at 5 p.m. of a late November afternoon.

Further, the basic rule is that the higher the magnification the narrower the field of view. Where the usual 2½X rifle scope, for example, will see at 100 yards a circle about 40 feet in diameter, the 4X sees only some 30 feet, and a 6X about 20 feet. Obviously, at some point an excess of magnification will make the scope hard to center on game quickly, especially if the deer is moving or is at short range.

ADVANTAGE OF SIMPLE CROSSHAIRS

For much the same reasons, the whitetail hunter is poorly served by a scope with a fine aiming point. A dot reticle covering anything smaller than a three-inch circle at 100

Three common types of reticules used in rifle scopes are the cross-hair, post, and dot. On long-range shots, the post or dot can obscure the target but they pay their own way on fast, close-in shooting

yards will disappear long before sunset. Even a six-inch dot is hard to find in a hurry. Crosshairs should span over one inch at 100 yards; a flat-topped post should measure off a full three inches at that range. Whether the hunter uses these basic reticle types or more complex multiple-post or tapering-crosshair designs is a matter of choice. The writer has long preferred simple coarse crosshairs because they are automatic, require no thought.

One gimmick particularly for the whitetail hunter: learn to use the scoped deer rifle as a shotgun. That is, learn to swing it to shoulder and point it with *both* eyes open at the buck, be he moving or standing. He will then appear in the center of your scope field. Some can actually shoot with both eyes open when using a low-X scope, but most probably will find it necessary to make the final aiming correction with the left or "off" eye winked shut.

This method is several times faster than raising the rifle with one eye shut and trying to find the buck through the limited field of the scope. It does take practice.

LONG-RANGE MULE SHOTS

Since the average range on shots at mule deer runs longer, out beyond 100 to as much as 300 to 400 yards, simply because they are more often hunted in relatively open terrain, the mule deer fancier selecting a scope can move up a stage or two in magnification and hence in seeing ability or resolving power.

While many who pursue the big-eared deer still swear by the basic 2½X scope, the majority go for 4X. Some—and these know that the circumstances of their particular hunting will call for long tries on standing game—use as high as 6X or even 8X. The western hunter can hardly go wrong, however, in plumping for a 4X. Its usual combination of a field about 30 feet across at 100 yards and hence 60 at 200, an exit pupil of roughly 8 mm. and a relative brilliance in the middle 60's, with weight and size factors reasonable to a sporting rifle, is just about right.

LENS REQUIRES TENDER CARE

It will cope nicely with running game at mountain-state distances, gives plenty of light for seeing during legal hunting hours, has resolution enough to make for accurate aiming over any range at which most of us should take shots at deer.

Hunters anywhere using rifle scopes of whatever type would do well to remember that scope caps protect lenses against dust and dirt as well as against rain or snow and there are snap-off types on the market. Lenses should not be scrubbed with a greasy shirttail but rather cleaned gently with tissue or dampened soft cloth. Scopes are not meant to drive nails with and should be treated with at least respect when the rifle is carried in truck or car. Fogging is more often the failure of the rifle-owner than of the scope in that he very likely left his musket in the hot and humid atmosphere behind the stove all night and then subjected it to sub-

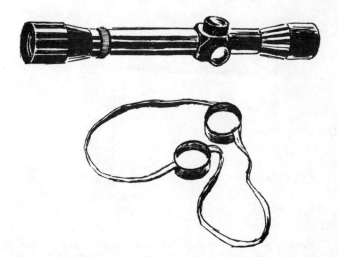

Hunters using rifle scopes of any type should remember to use scope caps to protect the lenses against dust, dirt, rain or snow

Fogged lenses of rifle scopes can be avoided by hanging gun under eaves of cabin at the end of the day rather than taking it inside where hot and humid atmosphere will lead to condensation on glass lenses during cooler hours next morning

zero cold next morning. Scopes are precision instruments and even if not actually fragile they should be treated as such.

WHEN TO USE BINOCULARS

Where the woods hunter after whitetail has little need for a spotting scope, he can use binoculars, especially if his rifle is rigged with a low-powered rifle scope. Not full-sized glasses, but pocket types rated at 6x24, 6x30 and so on, he will find very handy when he can see legs and a dim body shape, but can't quite be sure whether the deer actually carries antlers or is standing in scraggly dead brush that merely looks like a rack.

The mule deer operator, however, will find good spotting and viewing glassware worth its weight in gold. If he is a dyed-in-the-wool trophy hunter, there is no substitute for a first-quality spotting scope and tripod, preferably a tripod high enough to sit behind, less for locating deer than for studying antler length and conformation. Choose no more than 25X, and no less than 15, since too much power in the spotter makes it useless in bad light, and too little makes it no better than binoculars.

For most mule deer hunting, ideal binocular glasses range from 6x30 through 7x35, 8x30, to 9x35, and should be of the lightweight variety, under 24 ounces. The huge 7x50 glasses so useful to mariners weigh three pounds or more and leave a hunter round-shouldered. Magnifications over 9X are for most people impossible to hold with any useful degree of steadiness. Compromise light-weights of the 7x35 and 8x30 sorts give best service in virtually all mountain-state hunting.

CHAPTER **8**

On the Track of the Rack

The honest-to-gosh army of deer hunters that moves into the back country each fall—and it is larger in numbers than our peacetime military forces—is a body of men with mixed hopes and intentions. Some go deer hunting for social reasons, to be out with the boys as it were, but the main body splits into two clearly marked groups: the meat-hunters and the trophy-hunters.

The vast majority belong in the first category. They talk hopefully of big bucks, may even hunt selectively for the first few days of the season, but are generally well satisfied to take home a nice tender forkhorn. And satisfied they might be, since in the eastern whitetail states a success ratio of one deer for each eight or 10 hunters is about par for the course. Even in the prime mule deer areas, the batting average is usually only a point or two either way of .500. In Utah, a famous mule deer state, during the 1965 season, 171,460 hunters took 88,030 deer.

ROASTS VS. RECORDS

Not everybody bags venison under the best of circumstances, whether he is hunting for roasts or records. So the meat hunter, if we may apply the term loosely, has almost as much reason to be proud of his forkhorn as the trophy-seeker has for his hatrack-sized wall decoration.

The truly selective hunter, including that small inner group that hunts only for heads of Boone & Crockett quality and simply will not shoot at any lesser buck, operates according to a definite set of principles. And these may as well be applied to the chap who is essentially a meat hunter, yet gets his greatest personal satisfaction from bringing out of the woods a buck of such proportions as to arouse envy

The antlers of the individual white-tail deer may deviate somewhat in the number of tines, but two or three erect tines usually appear along the main beam as it makes a circular sweep

from his friends, even though the whopper may not make the official Boone & Crockett list.

STANDARD SYSTEM FOR TROPHIES

Before we get into those operating principles or methods, let's define terms. Many hunters are not familiar with the Boone & Crockett Club and its recording systems. The club

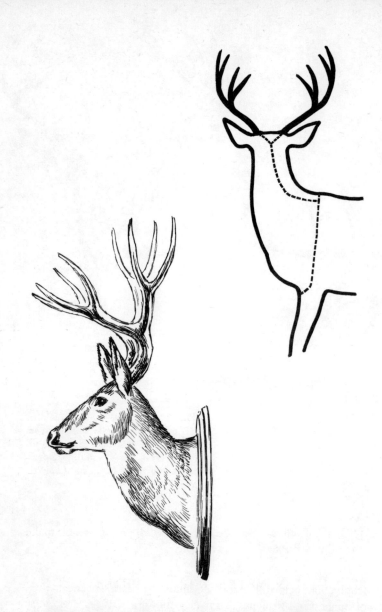

If you decide to mount the head and antlers as a trophy, make
a trophy cape cut along the top of the neck from a point just
behind withers, rather than up the throat from brisket

was formed in 1887 at the instigation of Theodore Roosevelt and is, not surprisingly, a group of sportsmen interested in conservation and in qualitative rather than quantitative hunting.

As early as 1932 it published classifications of trophies by Prentiss Gray under a standardized scoring system. By 1949, measurement methods had been established and have since been followed by repeated publication of "THE RECORDS OF NORTH AMERICAN BIG GAME" (most recently by Holt, Rinehart, Winston, Inc., New York City, in 1964) and by biennial competitions in the 29 categories of this continent's recognized game species.

Under the Official Scoring System, the worth of a deer head is not merely a factor of its extreme width or spread. Basically, the trophy is valued by a composite score involving the *inside* spread, the length of each beam, the length of each point, the circumferences of each beam between points, with debits for any differences between the right and left antlers.

WHERE TO GET FORMS

The same basic system is followed for whitetail and the related Coues deer of Arizona, for mule deer and the related Columbian blacktail of the northwestern states and Alaska. A separate and more complex scheme is used for the multiple-pointed, abnormal, or non-typical heads so common among both whitetail and mule deer.

The Secretary of the Boone & Crockett Club Records Committee, from whom measurement or competition entry blanks may be obtained, should be addressed at the Carnegie Museum, 4400 Forbes Avenue, Pittsburgh.

Official tapings must be done at least 60 days after the trophy has been taken in fair chase (without improper use of machines, airplanes, or other modern devices) by any one of a long list of qualified measurers, largely taxidermists, scattered over the United States.

The fostering of the Boone & Crockett idea of very se-

RECORDS OF NORTH AMERICAN BIG GAME COMMITTEE

BOONE AND CROCKETT CLUB

Boone and Crockett Club
Records of North American Big Game Committee
c/o Carnegie Museum
4400 Forbes Ave. Pittsburgh, Pa. 15213

MULE and BLACKTAIL DEER

KIND OF DEER _____

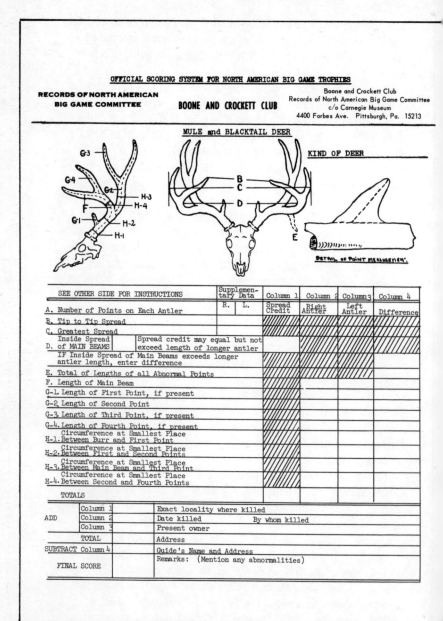

DETAIL OF POINT MEASUREMENT.

SEE OTHER SIDE FOR INSTRUCTIONS	Supplementary Data R.	Supplementary Data L.	Column 1 Spread Credit	Column 2 Right Antler	Column 3 Left Antler	Column 4 Difference
A. Number of Points on Each Antler			//////			
B. Tip to Tip Spread			//////	//////	//////	//////
C. Greatest Spread				//////	//////	//////
D. Inside Spread of MAIN BEAMS Spread credit may equal but not exceed length of longer antler				//////	//////	//////
IF Inside Spread of Main Beams exceeds longer antler length, enter difference			//////	//////	//////	
E. Total of Lengths of all Abnormal Points			//////	//////	//////	
F. Length of Main Beam			//////			
G-1 Length of First Point, if present			//////			
G-2 Length of Second Point			//////			
G-3 Length of Third Point, if present			//////			
G-4 Length of Fourth Point, if present			//////			
H-1. Circumference at Smallest Place Between Burr and First Point			//////			
H-2. Circumference at Smallest Place Between First and Second Points			//////			
H-3. Circumference at Smallest Place Between Main Beam and Third Point			//////			
H-4. Circumference at Smallest Place Between Second and Fourth Points			//////			
TOTALS						

ADD	Column 1		Exact locality where killed
	Column 2		Date killed By whom killed
	Column 3		Present owner
	TOTAL		Address
SUBTRACT Column 4			Guide's Name and Address
FINAL SCORE			Remarks: (Mention any abnormalities)

I certify that I have measured the above trophy on _____ 19 _____
at (address) _____ City _____ State _____
that these measurements and data are, to the best of my knowledge and belief, made in
accordance with the instructions given.

Witness:_____ Signature: _____

INSTRUCTIONS

All measurements must be made with a flexible steel tape to the nearest one-eighth of an
inch. Wherever it is necessary to change direction of measurement, mark a control point
and swing tape at this point. To simplify addition, please enter fractional figures in
eighths. Official measurements cannot be taken for at least sixty days after the animal
was killed. Please submit photographs.
Supplementary Data measurements indicate conformation of the trophy, and none of the
figures in Lines A, B and C are to be included in the score. Evaluation of conformation
is a matter of personal preference. Excellent, but nontypical Mule Deer heads with many
points shall be placed and judged in a separate class.
A. Number of Points on Each Antler. To be counted a point, a projection must be at least
one inch long AND its length must exceed the length of its base. All points are measured
from tip of point to nearest edge of beam as illustrated. Beam tip is counted as a point
but not measured as a point.
B. Tip to Tip Spread measured between tips of main beams.
C. Greatest Spread measured between perpendiculars at right angles to the center line of
the skull at widest part whether across main beams or points.
D. Inside Spread of Main Beams measured at right angles to the center line of the skull at
widest point between main beams. Enter this measurement again in "Spread Credit" column
if it is less than or equal to the length of longer antler.
E. Total of Lengths of all Abnormal Points. Abnormal points are generally considered to
be those nontypical in shape or location.
F. Length of Main Beam measured from lowest outside edge of burr over outer curve to the
tip of the main beam. The point of beginning is that point on the burr where the center
line along the outer curve of the beam intersects the burr.
G-1-2-3-4. Length of Normal Points. Normal points are the brow (or first) and the upper
and lower forks as shown in illustration. They are measured from nearest edge of beam
over outer curve to tip. To determine nearest edge (top edge) of beam, lay the tape
along the outer curve of the beam so that the top edge of the tape coincides with the
top edge of the beam on both sides of the point. Draw line along top edge of tape. This
line will be base line from which point is measured.
H-1-2-3-4. Circumferences - If first point is missing, take H-1 and H-2 at smallest place
between burr and second point. If third point is missing, take H-3 half way between the
base and tip of second point. If the fourth missing, take H-4 half way between the
second point and tip of main beam.

* * * * * * * * * * * * *

NO TROPHY OBTAINED BY UNFAIR CHASE MAY BE ENTERED
IN ANY BOONE AND CROCKETT BIG GAME COMPETITION

Spotting or herding Land game from the air, followed by landing in its vicinity for pursuit, shall be deemed UNFAIR CHASE and unsportsmanlike. Herding or pursuing ANY game
from motor powered vehicles shall likewise be deemed Unfair Chase and unsportsmanlike.

* * *

I certify that the trophy scored on this chart was taken in Fair Chase as defined above
by the Boone & Crockett Club. I certify that it was not taken by spotting or herding
from the air followed by landing in its vicinity for pursuit. I further certify that it
was not taken by herding or pursuing from motor powered vehicles and that it was taken
in full compliance with the local game laws of the province or state.

Date _____ Hunter _____
A-5M-9-65   (Written request for privilege of complete reproduction is suggested)

OFFICIAL SCORING SYSTEM FOR NORTH AMERICAN BIG GAME TROPHIES

**RECORDS OF NORTH AMERICAN
BIG GAME COMMITTEE**　　**BOONE AND CROCKETT CLUB**

Boone and Crockett Club
Records of North American Big Game Committee
c/o Carnegie Museum
4400 Forbes Ave.　Pittsburgh, Pa.　15213

WHITETAIL and COUES DEER

KIND OF DEER

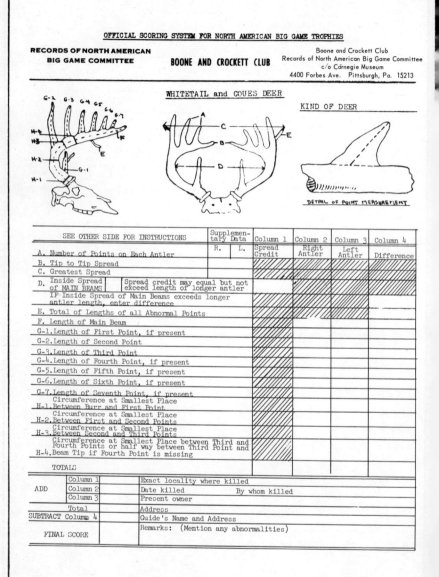

DETAIL OF POINT MEASUREMENT

SEE OTHER SIDE FOR INSTRUCTIONS	Supplementary Data		Column 1	Column 2	Column 3	Column 4
	R.	L.	Spread Credit	Right Antler	Left Antler	Difference
A. Number of Points on Each Antler						
B. Tip to Tip Spread						
C. Greatest Spread						
D. Inside Spread of MAIN BEAMS — Spread credit may equal but not exceed length of longer antler						
IF Inside Spread of Main Beams exceeds longer antler length, enter difference						
E. Total of Lengths of all Abnormal Points						
F. Length of Main Beam						
G-1. Length of First Point, if present						
G-2. Length of Second Point						
G-3. Length of Third Point						
G-4. Length of Fourth Point, if present						
G-5. Length of Fifth Point, if present						
G-6. Length of Sixth Point, if present						
G-7. Length of Seventh Point, if present						
H-1. Circumference at Smallest Place Between Burr and First Point						
H-2. Circumference at Smallest Place Between First and Second Points						
H-3. Circumference at Smallest Place Between Second and Third Points						
H-4. Circumference at Smallest Place between Third and Fourth Points or half way between Third Point and Beam Tip if Fourth Point is missing						
TOTALS						

ADD	Column 1		Exact locality where killed	
	Column 2		Date killed	By whom killed
	Column 3		Present owner	
	Total		Address	
SUBTRACT Column 4			Guide's Name and Address	
FINAL SCORE			Remarks: (Mention any abnormalities)	

I certify that I have measured the above trophy on _____ 19_____

at (address) _____

                City   State

and that these measurements and data are, to the best of my knowledge and belief, made in accordance with the instructions given.

Witness:_____ Signature: _____

INSTRUCTIONS

All measurements must be made with a flexible steel tape to the nearest one-eighth of an inch. Wherever it is necessary to change direction of measurement, mark a control point and swing tape at this point. To simplify addition, please enter fractional figures in eighths. Official measurements cannot be taken for at least sixty days after the animal was killed. Please submit photographs.

Supplementary Data measurements indicate conformation of the trophy, and none of the figures in Lines A, B and C are to be included in the score. Evaluation of conformation is a matter of personal preference. Excellent, but nontypical Whitetail Deer heads with many points shall be placed and judged in a separate class.

A. Number of Points on each Antler. To be counted a point, a projection must be at least one inch long AND its length must exceed the length of its base. All points are measured from tip of point to nearest edge of beam as illustrated. Beam tip is counted as a point but not measured as a point.

B. Tip to Tip Spread measured between tips of Main Beams.

C. Greatest Spread measured between perpendiculars at right angles to the center line of the skull at widest part whether across main beams or points.

D. Inside Spread of Main Beams measured at right angles to the center line of the skull at widest point between main beams. Enter this measurement again in "Spread Credit" column if it is less than or equal to the length of longer antler.

E. Total of Lengths of all Abnormal Points. Abnormal points are generally considered to be those nontypical in shape or location.

F. Length of Main Beam measured from lowest outside edge of burr over outer curve to the most distant point of what is, or appears to be, the main beam. The point of beginning is that point on the burr where the center line along the outer curve of the beam intersects the burr.

G-1-2-3-4-5-6-7. Length of Normal Points. Normal points project from main beam. They are measured from nearest edge of main beam over outer curve to tip. To determine nearest edge (top edge) of beam, lay the tape along the outer curve of the beam so that the top edge of the tape coincides with the top edge of the beam on both sides of the point. Draw line a-long top edge of tape. This line will be base line from which point is measured.

H-1-2-3-4. Circumferences - If first point is missing, Take H-1 and H-2 at smallest place between burr and second point.

*   *   *   *   *   *   *   *   *   *   *   *

NO TROPHY OBTAINED BY UNFAIR CHASE MAY BE ENTERED IN ANY BOONE AND CROCKETT BIG GAME COMPETITION

Spotting or herding Land game from the air, followed by landing in its vicinity for pursuit, shall be deemed UNFAIR CHASE and unsportsmanlike. Herding or pursuing ANY game from motor powered vehicles shall likewise be deemed Unfair Chase and unsportsmanlike.

*   *   *

I certify that the trophy scored on this chart was taken in Fair Chase as defined above by the Boone & Crockett Club. I certify that it was not taken by spotting or herding from the air followed by landing in its vicinity for pursuit. I further certify that it was not taken by herding or pursuing from motor powered vehicles and that it was taken in full compliance with the local game laws of the province or state.

Date _____ Hunter _____

A-5M-9-65

RECORDS OF NORTH AMERICAN BIG GAME COMMITTEE

BOONE AND CROCKETT CLUB

Boone and Crockett Club
Records of North American Big Game Committee
c/o Carnegie Museum
4400 Forbes Ave. Pittsburgh, Pa. 15213

NON-TYPICAL MULE DEER

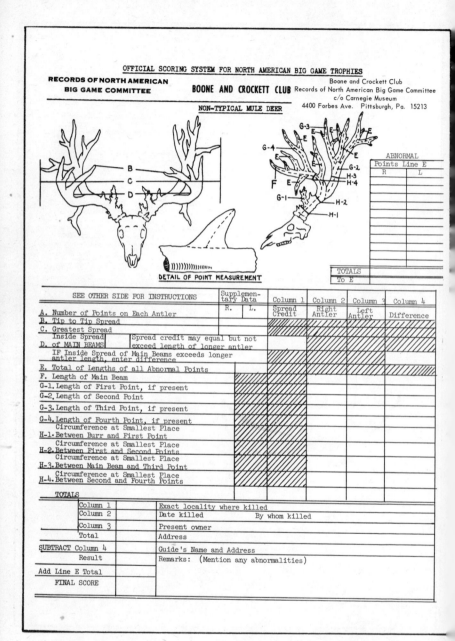

DETAIL OF POINT MEASUREMENT

ABNORMAL Points Line E

	R	L

| TOTALS To E | | |

SEE OTHER SIDE FOR INSTRUCTIONS	Supplementary Data		Column 1	Column 2	Column 3	Column 4
	R.	L.	Spread Credit	Right Antler	Left Antler	Difference
A. Number of Points on Each Antler						
B. Tip to Tip Spread						
C. Greatest Spread						
D. Inside Spread of MAIN BEAMS	Spread credit may equal but not exceed length of longer antler					
IF Inside Spread of Main Beams exceeds longer antler length, enter difference						
E. Total of Lengths of all Abnormal Points						
F. Length of Main Beam						
G-1. Length of First Point, if present						
G-2. Length of Second Point						
G-3. Length of Third Point, if present						
G-4. Length of Fourth Point, if present						
H-1. Circumference at Smallest Place Between Burr and First Point						
H-2. Circumference at Smallest Place Between First and Second Points						
H-3. Circumference at Smallest Place Between Main Beam and Third Point						
H-4. Circumference at Smallest Place Between Second and Fourth Points						

TOTALS		
Column 1		Exact locality where killed
Column 2		Date killed By whom killed
Column 3		Present owner
Total		Address
SUBTRACT Column 4		Guide's Name and Address
Result		Remarks: (Mention any abnormalities)
Add Line E Total		
FINAL SCORE		

96

**RECORDS OF NORTH AMERICAN
BIG GAME COMMITTEE**

BOONE AND CROCKETT CLUB

Boone and Crockett Club
Records of North American Big Game Committee
c/o Carnegie Museum
4400 Forbes Ave. Pittsburgh, Pa. 15213

☐ NON-TYPICAL WHITETAIL DEER Min. Score 160: 20=180
☐ Coues Deer Min. Score 105: 15=120 (NON-TYPICAL)

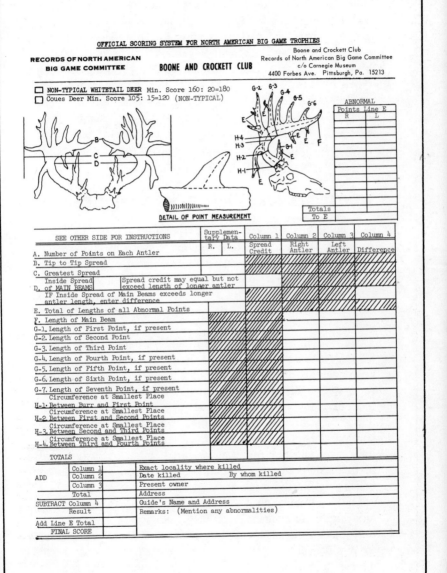

DETAIL OF POINT MEASUREMENT

ABNORMAL
Points Line E

	R	L
Totals		
To E		

SEE OTHER SIDE FOR INSTRUCTIONS	Supplementary Data		Column 1	Column 2	Column 3	Column 4
	R.	L.	Spread Credit	Right Antler	Left Antler	Difference
A. Number of Points on Each Antler						
B. Tip to Tip Spread						
C. Greatest Spread						
D. Inside Spread of MAIN BEAMS — Spread credit may equal but not exceed length of longer antler						
IF Inside Spread of Main Beams exceeds longer antler length, enter difference						
E. Total of Lengths of all Abnormal Points						
F. Length of Main Beam						
G-1. Length of First Point, if present						
G-2. Length of Second Point						
G-3. Length of Third Point						
G-4. Length of Fourth Point, if present						
G-5. Length of Fifth Point, if present						
G-6. Length of Sixth Point, if present						
G-7. Length of Seventh Point, if present						
H-1. Circumference at Smallest Place Between Burr and First Point						
H-2. Circumference at Smallest Place Between First and Second Points						
H-3. Circumference at Smallest Place Between Second and Third Points						
H-4. Circumference at Smallest Place Between Third and Fourth Points						
TOTALS						

ADD	Column 1		Exact locality where killed	
	Column 2		Date killed	By whom killed
	Column 3		Present owner	
	Total		Address	
SUBTRACT	Column 4		Guide's Name and Address	
	Result		Remarks: (Mention any abnormalities)	
Add Line E Total				
FINAL SCORE				

lective hunting by all serious outdoor publications has resulted in rapid growth of this philosophy among hunters and a tremendous lifting of the standards for record game. Not only have the various records for bear, moose, sheep, mountain lion and other such game types been repeatedly broken in modern times, but the quality of more common types, like elk, whitetail, and mule deer, of which hundreds of thousands are shot by sportsmen each fall, has been amazingly raised. During the year 1965, for example, one whitetail head was picked up, and one gargantuan buck shot by an Illinois archer, both of which broke the record of 202 points set by a deer killed back in 1918!

MINIMUM SCORES FOR DEER TROPHIES

It is the goal of every serious trophy hunter first to locate and then to take game that will make these listings. In the case of the deer types, with an annual kill of over 1,000,000 whitetail and over 600,000 muleys, the minimums for typical heads are scores of 160 and 185 points respectively. Such trophies require both good management and good luck.

Study of the whitetail records and of data in FIELD & STREAM'S Big Game Honor Badge records reveals that no longer do the super-whitetail come from traditional big rack states like Maine, Michigan, Pennsylvania, and the like. In many of these areas, though Maine regularly produces large-bodied deer hefting 300 pounds or more, a combination of hard hunting over many years, with bucks-only laws which have often resulted in an excessive herd of deer competing for limited feeding range, has produced bucks small in the rack.

Of late, midwestern states or farming areas where deer enjoy unlimited mineral-rich feed, and where seasons have only recently been opened after closures dating back prior to World War I, so that bucks have been able to grow old enough to reach true trophy size, have shown the greatest racks.

Any one careful enough to chart the origins of the record deer of this past generation also will discover that the area roughly 140 miles wide and half as deep stretching across the lower third of Saskatchewan is still productive of massive heads. Yet the finest buck the author ever shot, still high in the whitetail record list, was taken in New Jersey within two hours' travel of Times Square.

WHERE TO LOOK FOR TROPHIES

The trophy-devotee can continue this study down into the details of his own or his preferred hunting state, searching out information as to where the elements of ample feed, easy winters, light hunting pressure, and above all mineral-rich feed, produces the bone growth that is responsible for big racks.

The mule deer hunter must follow the same procedure in attempting to locate areas that tend to produce not only lots of deer, but also bucks with heavy and wide antlers. Study of the recent records and correspondence with guides and game officials will give him a lead, but half the hunting lies in this area search.

WHITETAIL SELECTION
REQUIRES QUICK DRAW

The whitetail aficionado has the greater problem when it comes to selection. Rarely, save in open-brush areas like those of Texas from Kerrville on the south and east can he leisurely examine a buck with binoculars, count points and estimate spread for trophy quality. The cover usually is too thick or the bucks move too fast.

In the section of Saskatchewan earlier referred to, hunting is usually done by driving the woodlots and windbreaks between farms, so the trophy-seeker must shoot now or hold his peace, guessing on the impression of an instant. Yet guess he must if he will not be happy with merely a fine eight or 10 point buck but must have one of Boone & Crockett quality.

By the very nature of his hunting terrain, the mule deer trophy hunter has better opportunity, especially if he can legally hunt his chosen area when the downhill migrations have started and the deer are moving toward the open semi-desert. Yet even then, and with the aid of binoculars and spotting scopes, selection is difficult.

RECORD DEER MAY BE SIZE OF ELK

All full-grown mule deer bucks, normally having four points and a brow prong on each side, look big. The record and near-record bucks look almost horrifyingly big, like bull elk. Seen from behind, a big muley's rack protrudes, or rather seems to protrude, eight inches to a foot beyond each side. If he is to hit the record book, the chances are he will appear, as he bounces off to leave you the poorest possible shot, wide enough to hang up in a garage door, even though the actual outside spread may be anywhere between 30 and 40 inches.

The trophy mule deer rack must seem astonishingly high, long in the prongs, at least twice—and better two and a half times—as high as his head is long. It must give an impression of great weight, since to be of record quality the beams just beyond the head must be in circumference at least 4½, or better, well over 5 inches, which is to say bigger around than the grip of your rifle.

Many hunters use the low-carried ears of an old muley as a gauge of his inside spread. As a general rule, the tip-to-tip width of those ears in normal stance is 21 to 22 inches, though those on the world's record typical muley (score 217) were only 20 inches. Hence, if from a straight-on front view it seems that the beams swing out beyond the ears, or the main stem of the two up-rearing top points on either side more than spans them, the inside spread will surely make the 23 to 30 inch measurement needed for possible record scoring.

BIG RACK OR SMALL DEER?

The body of the buck himself must of course be taken into consideration. If he is in poor condition, his rack is always going to seem oversize. The mule deer of the arid Big Bend country of southern Texas, small because of the battle they wage with poor feed, all seem to have gigantic antlers. Conversely, a Roman-nosed old buck who has lived beyond breeding age, has been fattened on the protein-rich grass of the timberline pastures, may be so big in body that his fine rack looks only ordinary.

But as a general rule to all mule deer trophy hunters—if a buck looks so big in the head that you at first think him an elk, if his rack causes you to goggle and gasp, shoot! Then get out the tape and find out the truth. If he didn't make it, plan on coming back again next year.

The dyed-in-the-wool big-rack hunter needs more patience than do his friends who are satisfied with just ordinary heads. He needs to put in more pre-season homework on where he should hunt, and how. He needs more restraint, to be dead-certain that he has not been misled by his own hopes. He needs a tape measure, one to be used on every trophy available to him, to help establish a set of personal standards. And above all, he needs a whole lawnful of four-leaf clovers!

CHAPTER 9

Dressing and Packing Out

The novice hunter standing over his first buck, flushed with honest excitement, his heart still pounding with the buck-fever jitters that happily occurred after the shot and not before, has every reason to be proud. In one sense he has fulfilled a man's destiny. And in about five minutes, after he has examined the buck's rack, patted himself on the back for placing his shot so well, he is due to fulfill another part of man's destiny—that of the dirty, and in some instances tough, job of dressing out his deer and somehow transporting the carcass back to camp or car.

One of the demands placed on young European hunters before they are fully licensed is to demonstrate skill in gutting out a deer or similar animal, utilizing only a pen knife or similar small-bladed knife, and bloodying their hands not at all beyond the wrist. This is quite possible, but rather an unnecessary refinement for our beginner hunter, though he should remember that the less mess he makes of his deer and of himself the more edible his meat is going to be.

SMALL KNIFE BETTER THAN MACHETE

The simplest start is at the stern. With the knife—and hunting knives with blades longer than four and a half to five inches or heavy enough to chop sugar cane are useless abominations—slit all the way around the outside of the anus, working the blade in deep as if coring an apple. The anus and its contents eventually will be removed either by splitting the pelvis of the buck, if it's a small one, or by pulling the anus up clear through the cut area and out with the abdominal contents if the buck is heavily boned.

Now skin off, being careful not to slash the knife point downwards into meat or abdomen, the testicles and penis,

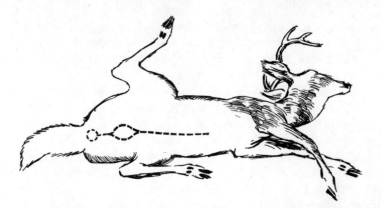

In dressing a deer, the simplest place to start is at the stern, cutting around the anus and the genitals. Then slip the knife through the peritoneum and forward so the abdomen is opened and the contents are free to fall out. But don't cut intestines

which can be removed in one tangle after the penis root has been snipped away from between the rump bulges.

DON'T PUNCTURE PAUNCH

Now, holding your forefinger along the back of the knife-blade cutting edge up, slip it through the peritoneum and work the edge forward so that the abdomen is opened and the entire contents are free to spill out. As the cut moves forward up to the brisket it may be necessary, on a big deer, to

When cutting abdomen of the deer hold forefinger along the back of the knifeblade. Small knives are easier to work with

reverse the cut and to make a down slash through the heavier hide and brisket hair. But under no circumstances should you let the knife point prick either coils of intestine or the bulging paunch.

Then, with sleeves rolled to the elbow, cut around the ribs where the diaphragm muscle is fastened like a curtain until it is free. Next reach in and up as far as possible with the left hand to grasp the windpipe. Cut it off. With one motion and with only a few obviously needed cuts you should now be able to roll out of the buck the entire body contents, from windpipe to anus.

Before wiping your hands on moss or grass, cut loose the liver and heart and place them on a handy rock or log to drain. Eventually you'll pack them into a plastic sack as the makings of tomorrow's breakfast. Then roll the buck over, open side down, so that all possible blood will drain from the body cavity.

WIPE, DON'T FLUSH, ABDOMINAL CAVITY

Clearly this job is most easily done if before starting the abdominal work you slide the buck around on his back so

If you have to leave the deer to get help in moving it, prop the belly open with a two-pointed stick to insure rapid cooling and proper drainage

The metatarsal gland of the white-tail is small, about one inch long, and located below mid-point of lower part of the leg

On the mule deer, the metatarsal glands are comparatively large, up to six inches in length. They are above mid-point

that his tail is pointed downhill and the forequarters are braced by a convenient log or rock. But the job can be done cleanly on flat ground. Once the gutting is accomplished, you should make every effort to get the buck into a draining position.

Do *not* flush out the abdomen, even if water is readily available. Instead, wipe it out with dry moss or grass, being careful to pick all possible meat-tainting hair off the exposed flesh. If you're going to have to leave the deer to get help, prop the belly cavity open with a two-pointed stick to ensure drainage and rapid cooling; and if it is to be left for long, get the carcass off the ground as much as possible.

The tarsal, or leg, glands most conspicuous on a mule deer's hind leg, inside and below the hock, are found on all three types of North American deer, and are the source of great argument. Do they or do they not taint the meat? Since they are easily sliced off, and smell pretty high when a buck is shot in mid-rut, the simplest answer is to remove them, wiping knife and hands clean after disposing of the glands.

You do *not* stick or slash the jugular vein for the purpose of bleeding out the meat. If your buck wasn't bled out beyond anything but a drip by your bullet some miracle has occurred, since dead animals don't bleed. Be sure also that you have skinned the buck no more than absolutely necessary—deer pack better and stay cleaner with the hair on.

MULEY CAN BE HOISTED ON POLES

You may decide to mount the buck's head and to take the trophy cape the basic skinning cut is forward, along the top of the neck, from a point just behind the withers, rather than forward up the throat from the brisket.

Most whitetail can be hauled by one man up over a few chunks of brush or a log so as to be left out over-night in cold weather, but a whopping muley might be another matter. To hoist him or any other heavy deer the very best answer is one of the two-pulley nylon cord hoists so widely sold. And the preferred position is head up. However, a determined man, alone, can get a big buck off the ground by

If a hunter must lift a large buck's carcass off the ground without help, he can do so by cutting three poles and lashing them together with the antlers at the center. Then he can work up one pole at a time until the deer has been lifted free

cutting three poles and tying them like ribs of a wigwam with the buck's antlers lashed to the center, then working up one pole at a time until the deer is lifted free.

Early in the season or in warm country, of course, the danger of having the meat fly-blown is so great that the buck should be wrapped in muslin or treated-paper fly bags as soon as possible, certainly before being left for any period of time. To facilitate this—and to make a deer easier to pack on a horse, take off the hind legs at the hock, and the forelegs at the knee, in both cases making your knife cuts from the outer side of the joint.

CARRY CARCASS LIKE BEDROLL

It's a rare hunter who at some time in his career isn't faced with the job of hauling out a buck that can't be reached by vehicle or pack horse. Nor does he have one of those bicycle-wheeled toters that would be so handy if they weren't 10 miles away at camp.

With a small whitetail, a husky man, under 45 and with no record of a heart condition, can tote the game out to the road. For an older man or one in poor condition this is folly. One accepted scheme is to tie the animal's legs together, being careful also to lash the head and antlers back out of the

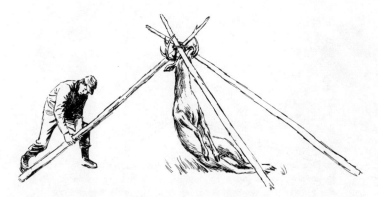

To carry a small whitetail carcass, tie the animal's four legs together and wear it like a Spanish War bedroll, with the hunter's head and shoulders inside the circle made by the bound deer. Author advises that the hunter decorate deer with bright bandannas for safety

A lone hunter also can remove a deer, especially if the ground is covered with snow, by lashing a length of wood through the antlers and using it as a handhold to drag the animal

With two men the straight drag with a long handhold tied to the antlers may be more effective than a pole or stretcher

way, then to wear it like a Spanish War bedroll, the hunter's head and shoulder inside the circle made by the bound deer. Whenever toting a deer the hunter is well advised to decorate it with bright red bandannas or to sing at least as loudly as the Seven Dwarfs!

A deer can be dragged by one man alone, especially if there has been a light fall of snow. There are two basic secrets to this method. First, use a short length of sapling as a handhold rather than the horns themselves, lashing it close so as to get as much of the buck's weight off the ground as possible. Second, always take the longer way around if that will avoid an uphill drag.

MAKE TRAVOIS FROM POLES

In some areas, if poles are available and the hunter has plenty of rope, he can make a sort of travois in which the whole buck is off the ground. The pole ends are placed over

If a couple of poles are available and the hunter has plenty of rope, he can make a travois for moving out the deer carcass. The pole ends are placed over the hunter's shoulders and only the points drag

Two men usually can carry a deer carcass tied to a single pole carried on their shoulders, but this method is not recommended

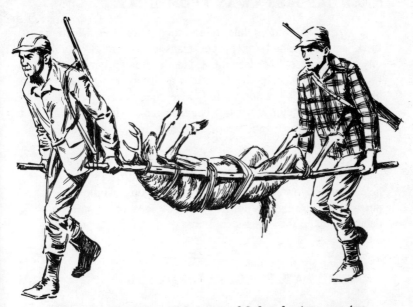

Another two-man carry for successful deer hunters uses two poles with the deer tied to the poles and toted between the hunters moving single file.

the hunter's shoulders and only the points drag. This device will make for easier going.

With two men, the straight drag with a longer handhold stick usually works better than either the two-pole hand carry, with the deer slung between the poles like a wounded soldier on a stretcher, or the one-pole shoulder carry, with the deer lashed to a single stout sapling and carried between the hunters moving single file. On rough ground and unless the two walkers can keep in broken rhythm, the one-pole carry is misery. Further—and this is true of any two-man system which can develop into a sort of blind rivalry—in dragging or carrying out a deer every modern hunter must be advised to pace himself. Five days a week at a desk or behind a counter is poor training for such effort.

KEEP CARCASS AWAY FROM HEAT

The modern automobile offers few places on which a buck can be lashed for proper transport. Carefully avoid any placement of the deer alongside the hood where it gets the full blast of engine heat, or into a closed trunk where it can be soured by a long trip. Once the buck has cooled properly, riding him on a top baggage rack, with a few bits of kindling placed underneath to insure full flow of air, is the best scheme.

If he must be carried inside, as in the bed of a station wagon, attention should likewise be paid to air flow, the car heater turned off if possible and the wagon's windows left partly open during any long stops. The idea in car-carrying deer is to keep the carcass cool, avoid meat contact with hot metal.

REMOVE FAT, PRESERVE FLAVOR

Venison is edible on the same day it is killed, the meat then having a taste sweeter than normal, but thereafter it should be left to hang for from four to eight days depending on the temperature. The 38 degrees usual in cooling rooms of a freezer plant is ideal for a week. Opinion is divided as to whether it is easier to skin a buck fresh or aged, but it is certainly more trouble if the whole animal has been frozen.

If you do your own butchering, common sense indicates treating the carcass as if it were a small beef animal, but on game of this sort careful removal of all suety fat is desirable before cooking, since the strong taste some deplore is found chiefly in the fat. And if you have the local freezer plant butcher and portion your buck into freezer packages, make sure that all the roasts, double-thick chops and steaks are deposited in your own locker!

CHAPTER 10

Clothing, Gear, and Gimmicks

Very possibly the finest mule .deer head I ever saw was shot by a Colorado rancher's son off a hay-stack. It's dollars to doughnuts that the farm boy who clobbered that monster buck gave no thought whatever to his hunting clothing. He just sneaked out behind the barn in his Levi's and flat-heeled work boots, thumbed his Stetson back out of his eyes, and let fly. Matter of fact, for about 87.4 percent of all mule deer hunting, he was pretty well outfitted.

The whitetail operator, however, is up against another set of circumstances. And the successful whitetail hunter must pay considerable attention to what he puts on. He may well face the bone-stiffening cold of long hours on a stump. Or he may be a ridge-climbing brushbuster and so suffer more from heat than from cold. And above all, whichever sort of whitetail hunter he may be, he will—or certainly should—wear clothing designed for quiet in the woods.

DEER COLOR-BLIND, BUT NOT DEAF

Hard-shelled poplins, canvas, or plastic materials are poor choices for the whitetail hunter. No matter how resistant they are to cold, wind, or wet, all the hard-shelled materials whistle. A twig slatting across the harsh surface of a canvas jacket, like a duck-shooting coat, is as much warning to a cautious old whitetail as is the multiple click of a hammer being cocked. And the Nimrod does not live who can Indian through the woods without rubbing his clothing against the branches.

At least the outer layer of the whitetail hunter's outfit

113

must be wool, or very soft-tanned leather like suede. And considering the factors of warmth and dampness, wool is the better choice. Under that he can wear anything he prefers, from a gold lamé undershirt to the stuffing out of a down pillow, but the outside should be quiet wool.

WEAR MULTI-LAYER CLOTHING

The great secret of keeping comfortable in woods clothing, of course, is to use the multiple layer principle. Two

Hunters planning long treks into unfamiliar country should carry a survival kit in case they become lost and have to spend a night in the woods. A compass, topographic maps, emergency rations, matches, a light axe, rain parka or tarpaulin, and light nylon rope should be included

medium shirts are always warmer than one heavy shirt because between them they trap a layer of insulating, dead air. By the same token, a sweater or insulated vest added under a medium jacket will probably give greater warmth than just a heavy jacket. Certainly it will offer far greater flexibility. As the sun warms things up around noon, or as you puff and sweat up a long hill, with multiple layers you can always strip off a thickness or two, if only to prevent becoming damp from perspiration. And you can slip it back on again should you sit for a while or the day turn colder.

The modern synthetic insulants have helped, oddly enough, to foster the multiple-layer approach to comfort. They are still hardly as warm, ounce for ounce, as honest goose down, but a hard-shelled down jacket is too noisy to be of use to the average whitetail hunter. Today's insulated underwear tops and vests and jacket liners of assorted synthetic materials are light, cheap, and lend themselves to handy stuffing into game pocket or knapsack during the warmer hours. Just remember to wear wool on the outside.

BOOTS FOR DEER HUNTERS

The sensible whitetail operator will own more than one type of hunting boot. If he hunts in the near-zero temperatures of late November or early December along the northern tier of deer states, particularly if he is a stump-sitter, the all-rubber insulated boot, 10 inches high, is unbeatable —awkward and heavy though they be for hiking long distances. Insulated leather boots run lighter on the foot, are far easier to walk in, and work just as well in dry snow. But leather cannot be expected, no matter what processing is used, to stay absolutely waterproof forever, certainly not in wet snow. Once the spongy insulation has soaked up water such boots are very slow to dry out. One comfortable old standby type is the all-leather unlined moccasin, still useful in fairly easy going.

Of course, deer hunters in wooded areas would feel com-

Several types of hunting boots are available for various kinds of terrain and weather. The all-rubber insulated boot, 10 inches high, is recommended for stump-sitters. Insulated leather boots may be preferred for long hunts on foot. Maine-type hunters use rubber-bottomed leather-topped pacs

pletely handicapped were they unable to buy the rubber-bottomed, leather-topped pacs which are synonymous with Maine deer hunting. They are still eminently practical in damp going, certainly until the weather becomes sharply cold.

SILK SOCKS PREVENT BLISTERS

There are tricks to getting the most from any boot. First off, two pairs of medium wool socks are more comfortable than one set of heavy ones, and on feet left tender by our civilized non-walking lives, a pair of silk socks under all helps prevent blistering. Second, properly chosen insoles not only help guard heels and arches against stone-bruising, but also raise the warmth coefficient of any boot.

The modern plastic insoles, which absorb no moisture at all, require no extra dry pair for a change. They set up an insulating dead air space between sock and boot sole. If you prefer sheepskin insoles, then wear them with the wool side down, smooth leather side up, and you'll no longer be troubled by crawling socks.

Most states today require of the deer hunter the wearing of red, yellow, or flame-orange in some minimum amount as identification to other hunters. Of the three colors, flame-orange is probably the most highly visible under all woods conditions. None of the three, by themselves, is visible to deer. Like nearly all game animals, deer are color blind. In fact, deer frequently will walk into yardstick range of a red-coated hunter, so long as he remains immobile and they do not catch his scent. But the fluorescent quality of some coloring does seem to catch the animal eye almost as quickly as it does the human. And it becomes markedly visible to both if there is perceptible movement. Blind reliance on bright colors as protection against those few idiots in the deer woods who cannot wait to surely spot doe from buck and man from either is a fallacy, anyway.

The accomplished deer hunter is he who so proceeds that he sees every other hunter first!

MULE DEER WARDROBE DIFFERENT

The mule deer Nimrod can wear whatever best suits him to the climate. Ordinarily his final stalk is conducted at enough distance so that whistling britches or the slat of brush on hard cloth makes no difference. And in much mule deer terrain, the need for bright red as human identification is less pronounced because there are fewer hunters per square mile. He is well advised to comply with any state requirement for wearing red, however. On one item the muley operator may differ—if he is foot-hunting in rugged country his boots should be fitted with soles of vibram or carry some similar cleating for sure-footed climbing through rocky ravines.

And of course the mule deer hunter traditionally wears a Stetson, in contrast to the cap, usually of wool, affected by the man in whitetail country. Presumably the wide-brimmed hat is the ultimate in keeping the bright western sun from a man's eyes, in fending off brush, and in keeping rainwater off a rider's neck; though it must be confessed that in this scrivener's experience the bill of a cap is better against sun. Big hats are forever being knocked off in brush, and no hat keeps your neck as dry as the hood of a rain parka. But in mule deer country, by all means wear a Stetson, with a red bandana worked under the band. Otherwise that big muley buck might feel slighted.

FOLDING SAW HELPFUL

The whitetail hunter has no need to sag his belt with a heavy hunting knife. It will gut his buck no more quickly or cleanly than a shorter, lighter blade. And seldom is there need to split a whitetail's pelvis or to quarter the buck in getting out the carcass. The mule deer fan may have some justification for a heavy bladed knife if he plans to quarter or halve a buck for packing. But a folding saw or even a light belt-axe will do a far better and quicker job, and will

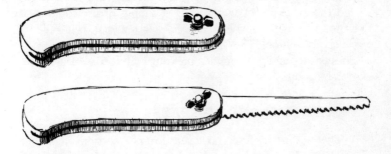

Whitetail hunters seldom need cutting tools heavier than a good knife but mule deer sometimes require quartering or at least pelvis splitting in the field in order to pack out the meat. For such jobs, a light belt-axe and a folding saw are more practical than a machete-sized knife

be vastly more useful should either hunter face a night out and the necessity of working up a supply of firewood. And as for hanging a revolver and holster on your belt—this is sheer affectation. The six-gun can never do what your rifle does easily, and four pounds on your belt at 6 A.M. will feel like 14 pounds come 6 P.M.

CARRY MAP AND COMPASS

There is no excuse, however, for not carrying a simple compass. If you also pocket a topographical map of the area, the compass and common sense will prevent your becoming lost. Even without the map, an operating compass can prevent a man's becoming seriously confused. In only the wildest country today can it be very many miles to the road that runs west of your hunting area, or to the valley that if you follow it in a southerly direction, will bring you down to the river and so somewhere near camp.

A precise map, a knowledge of compass declination and map usage, and the ability to recognize landmarks from the back or usually unseen side—these are the signs of the experienced woodsman. But even the ordinary bloke, if he keeps his head and uses his compass should never become seriously lost.

And should that disaster occur, the intelligent man will not try to fight his way out through a trackless swamp or limitless tangle of blowdowns. That's the way to break a leg or become even more badly confused.

The sensible man will stay put. As darkness approaches he'll lay in a supply of dry wood, at least enough for the whole night, will prepare himself to siwash it under a heavy spruce, or against a heat-reflecting rock.

Morning will bring a fresh light on matters, and certainly will permit his companions time to organize a planned search. With a fire and half a candy bar left over from lunch, a lost hunter is in far better shape than he is blundering about in the dark, perhaps falling off a cliff.

ITEMS FOR SURVIVAL KIT

Few whitetail hunters push back in far from the roads, anyway, the average being less than a mile. But those who do strike off into remote areas are well advised to use a small knapsack or light packboard as a day pack. It will take, without discommoding the carrier, those handy items that will make life easier and might mean the difference between life and death. The pack can contain extra socks, a light silk-and-neoprene rain parka or a poncho that can double as a tarpaulin, a bit of candle for fire lighting in the rain, a light axe, a plastic bag for deer liver and heart, a meal or so of dried or compacted food, a few yards of light nylon rope, an extra shirt if you're in country where marked temperature drop is likely—as well as the steel tape and camera that will forever immortalize the huge buck you're heading so far back in for.

Cartridge and Bullet Weight	100 Yds.	Trajectory Peak
.243-100	+ 3″	3.3″ @ 180
.244-90	+ 3″	3.4″ @ 180
.257-100	+ 3″	3.3″ @ 150
.257-117	+ 3″	3.0″ @ 125
.264-140	+ 3″	3.5″ @ 170
.270-130 (& .280-125)	+ 3″	3.4″ @ 170
.270-150	+ 3″	3.1″ @ 140
.280-150	+ 3″	3.2″ @ 140
.30-06-150	+ 3″	3.2″ @ 150
.30-06-180	+ 3″	3.0″ @ 125
.30-06-220	+ 3″	3.2″ @ 115
.300 H & H-180	+ 3″	3.2″ @ 140
.308-150	+ 3″	3.0″ @ 150
.300 WM-180	+ 3″	3.4″ @ 170
7 M/M Mag.-160	+ 3″	3.4″ @ 170
.30-30-170 RN	+ 1.5″	1.5″ @ 90
.35 Rem.-200 RN	+ 1.5″	1.6″ @ 90
.358 Win.-200	+ 3″	3.0″ @ 100
.375 H & H-270	+ 3″	3.0″ @ 150

SIGHTING BY RULE OF THREE

The Rule of Three table is based on the premise that with modern cartridges, generally operating at velocities between 2500 and 3200 feet per second, zeroing a scope-sighted hunting rifle so that the center of impact at 100 yards is three inches above the point of aim gives practical peak effectiveness for both rifle and cartridge. The rifle is then **targeted for** a range between 200 and 300 yards, the exact range depending on velocity, bullet weight, and shape.

The bullet rises only fractionally more than three inches

Targeted or (Yds.)	Hold Dead On To	Hold Over 12" At
275	325	400
275	325	400
230	270	350
200	240	310
300	340	425
265	310	400
215	255	330
240	290	375
245	285	370
215	260	340
190	230	300
250	290	370
230	275	350
290	325	400
290	325	400
150	180	250
150	180	240
195	230	300
220	260	340

above line of sight, drops back through that line, and by the time it has dropped three inches below the line of sight it has reached a range close to the maximum distance for dead-sure expansion of most bullets. That range we call the effective point-blank range.

We can hold **dead on** our game to that distance because the bullet will rise and fall only three inches off the line of sight. And in practical hunting, the game's vital area is at least six inches in diameter.

Few hunters can hold inside six inches beyond a distance of 200 yards. But the table has been carried out to give the range at which he should hold over one foot. For most modern loads, the one-foot hold over distance is between 250 and 400 yards and few hunters can judge greater distances accurately.

The first column in the table lists the cartridge and the bullet weight in grains. Except for those marked RN (round nose), the bullets are assumed to be at least as well shaped as Winchester-Western Silvertips or Remington Cor-Lokt.

The second and third columns show the amount of rise above the line of sight that can be expected during the particular bullet's trajectory at distances of 50 and 100 yards. Some will rise and then fall below the line of sight more rapidly than others which have a flatter trajectory. The fourth column shows the trajectory peak, or the highest point above the line of sight that will be reached by the bullet before it begins to drop towards the earth. The .243-100, for example, will peak at 3.3 inches above the line of sight at 180 yards.

To use the table, zero your rifle and hunting load to hit three inches up at 100 yards. Then memorize only the "Hold Dead On" and "Hold Over 12" yardages for that load. Forget other trajectory factors as merely confusing matters. If your pet cartridge is not listed, pick the one nearest to it in velocity and bullet weight, adjusting the yardages slightly as the relative speeds indicate. In other words, for the 180-grain .308 Winchester load use the 180-grain .30-06 data and reduce the ranges by 10 to 20 yards, which is not enough to upset matters when you are shooting under hunting conditions. If you shoot handloads, the small speed difference will mean little change.

Information in the tables is based on calculations, with exact yardages rounded off for practical use.

WIND DRIFT IN INCHES

The effect of wind may make long shots at game more difficult than does trajectory drop

10 mph wind at 3 or 9 o'clock

Cartridge	100 yds	200 yds	300 yds
.22 Long Rifle (Match)	3.6		
.22 Long Rifle (40 gr. @ 1835 f.p.s.) High Velocity	·5.0	17.1	
.222 Rem. (50 @ 3200)	1.6	7.2	17.8
.220 Swift (48 @ 4100)	1.4	6.4	15.8
.243 WFC (80 @ 3500)	1.1	4.0	10.0
.257 (87 @ 3200)	1.2	4.9	11.0
.264 WFC (140 @ 3200)	.7	3.1	7.0
.264 WFC (100 @ 3200)	.9	3.9	9.2
.30-06 (172 @ 2700)	.7	2.6	6.0

A 5-mile wind causes about half as much drift as a 10-mile wind; a 20-mile breeze, enough to sway trees actively, twice as much. Winds from other angles have varied effects, about 50 percent from 1, 5, 7, 11 o'clock and 87 percent from 2, 4, 8, and 10 o'clock.

A lone hunter sometimes can get his deer by figuring out just where the buck would be bedded down—over the nose of a ridge from which he can see in several directions, over which flow the air currents that carry danger signals, and from which he can escape quite easily

RIFLE RECOIL

The recoil energy of a rifle can be calculated by a mathematical formula which is rather complicated but includes the weight of the rifle, the weight of the bullet, the weight of the powder charge, and the muzzle velocity of the bullet. And, because of other factors, the results are approximate.

Cartridge	Rifle Weight (lbs.)	Recoil Energy (ft. lbs.)
.222 Rem. (50 gr @ 3200 f.p.s.)	7.0	3.50
.243 Win. (100 @ 3070)	6.5	12.50
.257 Rob. (117 @ 2650)	8.0	9.00
.264 Win. (140 @ 3200)	8.0	20.50
.270 Win. (130 @ 3140)	8.0	16.50
7m/m Mag. (160 @ 3100)	8.5	23.00
.300 H & H Mag. (180 @ 2920)	8.0	26.50
.300 Wea. Mag. (180 @ 3300)	8.5	35.00
.30-06 (180 @ 2700)	8.0	20.00
.308 Win. (180 @ 2610)	6.5	22.00
.338 Win (250 @ 2700)	9.0	29.00
.375 H & H (300 @ 2550)	9.0	44.00
.458 Win. (500 @ 2125)	9.5	65.00

Guns should never be taken out of the car with the barrel toward any person and they should be carried in a car both cased and empty

POCKET GLOSSARY

Ballistics. The study of projectiles in flight is called exterior ballistics; that of actions incidental to firing within the gun, interior ballistics.

Bore Diameter. The measurement across the tops of the opposite lands, or surfaces between grooves, within the rifled bore. Usually .300 in a .30-caliber barrel.

Caliber. Sometimes stated as bore dimension, sometimes as groove dimension, sometimes as neither, as in .222 Remington. May also use a proprietary name (as H & H), date of adoption (as .30-06,) or in the case of black powder cartridges, powder charge in grains (as .45-70).

Cannelure. A rolled-in ring around a bullet body to serve as a crimping ring or to bind in the lead core. Also, the groove above the case head.

Drift. The small movement of a bullet to the right or the left of the bore line due to the effect of its spin. Also, commonly used in respect to windage.

Erosion. The washing away, by heat and gas-blasted powder grains, of the throat section of a rifle barrel. It is more pronounced in large-charge, high intensity combinations and least with small powder charges or guns with large bores.

Groove Diameter. The distance across the bottoms of opposite grooves, often .003 to .008 greater than the bore diameter.

Muzzle Energy and Velocity. Calculated ballistic data derived from instrumental velocity data taken at distances of five to 50 feet from the muzzle.

Reticle. The cross-hairs, post, dot, or other system within a telescopic sight for focussing on a target.

Trajectory. The path traced by a bullet from the muzzle to the point of impact.

Zero. In common usage, the sight setting which will enable the rifleman to place his bullet where he wants it to hit, as precisely as the rifle permits.

ABOUT THE ARTISTS

Richard Amundsen, who painted the cover illustration for FIELD & STREAM Guide to Deer Hunting, was born in California in 1928 and lived in San Francisco until 1960 when he moved to the state of Washington. When he is not illustrating covers and stories for national magazines, Amundsen works as an artist for a number of advertising accounts and trains retrievers.

Mort Kunstler, who illustrated the inside pages of the Guide to Deer Hunting, was an outstanding New York area athlete before turning to a career of illustrating magazines and books. He was the first Brooklyn College student to become a four-letter man, then transferred to U.C.L.A. and the Pratt Institute. Kunstler, with his wife and three children, recently returned to the New York area after living several years in Mexico. They make their home at Oyster Bay Cove, Long Island.